If you are a parent of young children, ... w
you truly wise ways to greater loving e...

—**Jack Kornfield, PhD**, author ...

"Need a quick reminder about how t... ve
time to read another book? Hunter created a handy compendium for you. Short
chapters with summaries and references to many of the strategies and skills you
read about when you *did* have time to read!"

—**Joanna Faber & Julie King**, coauthors of the best-selling books, *How to Talk So Little Kids Will Listen* and *How to Talk When Kids Won't Listen*

"Hunter is all at once the science-based professional, the friend who shares and validates life in the parenting trenches, and the practical coach giving immediately actionable advice. In brilliant short-take form, this book guides parents to start with ourselves—regulating our own stress responses and reactivity—and to practice what our kids need most from us: authentic, 'good enough' parenting."

—**Tina Payne Bryson, LCSW, PhD**, *New York Times* bestselling coauthor of *The Whole-Brain Child* and *No-Drama Discipline*, and author of *The Bottom Line for Baby*

"Hunter understands that parents need a combination of information, inspiration, compassion, and action. Reading this book is like having by your side a smart parenting expert, an inspiring role model, a compassionate friend, and a firm but loving coach—all rolled into one."

—**Lawrence J. Cohen, PhD**, psychologist, author of *Playful Parenting*, and coauthor of *Unplug and Play*

"Hunter Clarke Fields has done it again! With her trademark humor and humility, she gently and generously shares her wisdom and experience alongside reflections and practices that point us back to our values that we hope to live and parent by. As you raise good humans in your children, you'll find yourself compassionately reparenting yourself to be the best you can be on this journey."

—**Christopher Willard, PsyD,** faculty at Harvard Medical School, and author of *Growing Up Mindful* and *Alphabreaths*

"Hunter has packed so much wisdom, humor, and kindness into each of these brief, readable chapters. This is the perfect read for parents who may not have the time or energy to read an entire parenting book—which, let's be honest, is all of us!"

—**Carla Naumburg, PhD**, author of *How to Stop Losing Your Sh*t with Your Kids*

"The giant gap between the parents we want to be and the parents we are when the kids are whining, fighting, and suddenly not tired at 9 pm is where this book lands us. Luckily, it proceeds to take us by the hand and lead us to the other side, which is still not perfect. But it sure is a lot calmer and happier. What a ride and what a guide!"

—**Lenore Skenazy**, president of Let Grow, and author of *Free-Range Kids*

"If you are a parent whose secret prayer is to be a better parent, *Raising Good Humans Every Day* offers an answer to your prayer. With humor, wisdom, and compassion, Hunter Clarke-Fields helps us calm our reactivity, and understand ourselves and our children much better. With each soothing, brief, readable chapter, you'll learn something to help improve your parenting and let go of some guilt. Keep this one within an arm's reach."

—**Rev. Iyanla Vanzant**, author of *Spiritual Life Coach*

"Parenting mindfully is deeply challenging. Thankfully, Hunter Clarke-Fields makes raising good humans both simple and accessible. With dozens of easy-to-implement tools, *Raising Good Humans Every Day* is an invaluable resource you will lean on and learn from again and again."

—**Shonda Moralis, MSW, LCSW**, author of *Breathe, Mama, Breathe*; and *Don't Forget to Breathe*

"A mindful parenting encyclopedia of sorts—Clarke-Fields's personal anecdotes offer readers tender support for those difficult and lonely moments, backed with the knowledge and expertise to truly foster confidence, connection, and transformation."

—**Sharon Salzberg,** author of *Lovingkindness* and *Real Life*

RAISING GOOD HUMANS EVERY DAY

50 Simple Ways to Press Pause, Stay Present & Connect with Your Kids

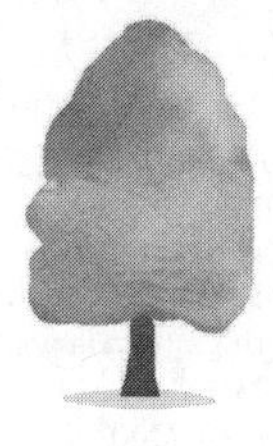

Hunter Clarke-Fields, MSAE

New Harbinger Publications, Inc.

Publisher's Note

This publication is designed to provide accurate and authoritative information in regard to the subject matter covered. It is sold with the understanding that the publisher is not engaged in rendering psychological, financial, legal, or other professional services. If expert assistance or counseling is needed, the services of a competent professional should be sought.

NEW HARBINGER PUBLICATIONS is a registered trademark of New Harbinger Publications, Inc.

New Harbinger Publications is an employee-owned company.

New Harbinger Publications, Inc.
5674 Shattuck Avenue
Oakland, CA 94609
www.newharbinger.com

Cover design by Sara Christian; Acquired by Elizabeth Hollis Hansen;
Edited by Kristi Hein

Library of Congress Cataloging-in-Publication Data

Names: Clarke-Fields, Hunter, author.
Title: Raising good humans every day : 50 simple ways to press pause, stay present, and connect with your kids / Hunter Clarke-Fields.
Description: Oakland, CA : New Harbinger Publications, 2023. | Includes bibliographical references.
Identifiers: LCCN 2023002872 | ISBN 9781648481420 (trade paperback)
Subjects: LCSH: Parenting. | Child rearing. | Parent and child.
Classification: LCC HQ755.8 .C546 2023 | DDC 649/.1--dc23/eng/20230406
LC record available at https://lccn.loc.gov/2023002872

MIX
Paper from responsible sources
FSC® C011935
FSC www.fsc.org

Printed in the United States of America

25 24 23

10 9 8 7 6 5 4 3 2 1 First Printing

I dedicate this book to my parents, grandparents, ancestors, and future generations. May we continue to evolve our understanding and compassion for what it means to be human.

Contents

Foreword

There isn't a parent in the world who doesn't feel lost and helpless—at times (or all the time). It's one thing to raise our kids and quite another to raise them *consciously*. Ah, this is a whole other kettle of fish indeed! Conscious parenting requires an elevated degree of awareness and insight that parents often find extremely challenging to implement in reality. How does a conscious parent show up in the nitty-gritty of everyday life? How do we consciously resolve conflicts with our teens without losing our minds? Or, how do we consciously manage our toddler's meltdowns without acting like one ourselves? If only our kids came with easy instructions, we wouldn't struggle with parenting them to the degree that we do. This is where this amazing book enters the picture to help us parents navigate the oft-treacherous tides of raising our children.

In this brilliant and insightful book, Hunter lays out the foundational strategies we need in order to better manage ourselves so we can better raise our kids. She takes extremely complex ideas and breaks them down into digestible, bite-size chapters that allow us to absorb them with ease and comfort. In addition, she has many practice exercises that allow us to take these ideas out of the realm of theory and into the real world so we can use them in daily action.

Some of the most effective lessons throughout the book are those centered around mindfulness, which I talk about as one of the key concepts in conscious parenting. Until and unless we parents can become more mindful and aware of ourselves, we will not be able to raise our children consciously. The reason mindfulness is so powerful is because it teaches us to pause before we react and use the space this provides to reflect on ourselves with courageous transparency. Hunter's expertise in teaching us mindfulness skills is apparent through this book and will give us all the salve we need as we find ourselves lost in the parenting sea.

In all my books on conscious parenting, the one common thread has been honest self-reflection. Each of the fifty succinct chapters in this book also leads us toward deeper self-appraisal and accountability. Hunter helps us confront our greatest fears and guilt as parents with compassion and humor, allowing us to look at ourselves in the mirror with acceptance and love. Her own stories along the path of conscious parenting help us realize that we are not alone in our mistakes or meltdowns. In fact, in a poignant way, Hunter allows us to feel empowered through our past errors and teaches us to use these "glitches" as fertile ground for transformation and growth. In all sorts of ways, we are led back to ourselves with grace and redemption.

There are few parenting books that hit the mark, and this one certainly does. With its calm reminders on how to stay in the present moment and its effective strategies on how to communicate and connect better with your kids, this book is an invaluable go-to to help you navigate the toughest moments of parenting. Thank you, Hunter, for giving us yet another enriching book to help all of us parents remember that we are human after all, and deserving of great heartfelt compassion for what we are trying to do.

I highly recommend that you keep this book by your bedside to help with those moments in parenting when you wonder how you will make it through another day. It will not only boost you with just the right amount of courage and wisdom, it will also allow you to do so with patience, humor, and confidence.

—Dr. Shefali Tsabary
Author of *The Conscious Parent* and *The Awakened Family*

Introduction: Parenting Is H.A.R.D.

Parents feel overstretched, overcommitted, underprepared, and underappreciated. —Hal Runkel

Parenting is *hard* for all of us. From the loneliness to the stress, spending lots of time with our little ones can be physically, mentally, and psychologically exhausting. Although adorable, our kids can be so messy, thoughtless, relentlessly whiney, and loud that sometimes we want to crawl into a corner and hide. In the Western world, we live as nuclear families, without a tribe of extended family—often, even without nearby friends—to support us. One parent is often left as the only adult, home alone with one or more little humans: a recipe for stress, unhappiness, and instability.

I found myself more or less in that position when my daughter was eighteen months old. My husband was working full time, and I'd elected to stay home with our child. My parents were a seven-hour drive away, so most of the time it was up to me to raise my daughter to be the best she could be. My job was to make sure that she was healthy, thriving, and happy. To be a good parent, I was supposed to give her the best foods for her growing body, to play with her and read to her, to ensure that she felt secure—to be there for her day and night, instilling the confidence and self-esteem so vital to living a good life.

I intended to be loving, connected, and kind, but firm. I would communicate calmly and skillfully, offering my child my best self. I envisioned that she would respond to this loving treatment with smiles and easy cooperation. We would embody an ideal social media mom-post: holding hands as she smiled up at me lovingly. I would feel nothing but ease, love, and joy as a parent.

The reality of parenting slapped me in the face. My daughter was fussy as a baby and highly sensitive to changes in her environment. She cried and fussed a lot. As a toddler she let me know that she did not like my parenting style (the "firm" part) with some big, loud "no's" and crying. Despite my best intentions, I found myself triggered, intensely frustrated, and shouting at her. I scared her. Seeing the fear and resistance in her eyes, I felt ashamed and guilty for not meeting my own expectations.

Far from being calm, I was filled with anxiety. I was scared that I was fundamentally messing up my precious child. Wasn't it up to me to ensure that she was secure and happy? Yet here I was doing exactly the opposite because of my temper. Was I irrevocably damaging my child? Would she always be so resistant? Was I doomed to repeat the combative, difficult relationship I'd had with my own father?

You may have similar fears. We've been told how important the early years are. We know that parenting can make a big difference to an individual's health, happiness, and well-being. Yet for many of us—largely alone with a small human for hours and hours—that pressure leads to anxiety and overwhelming stress.

If you saw a job posting for a position that promised yelling, crying, and attitude from your coworkers, isolation, never-ending mess, and outsized responsibility, twenty-four hours a day with no breaks *ever*, you would probably run for the hills! Yet social media tells us we *should* feel blissful—with an unwavering sense of deep fulfillment from parenting. Older people tell us to "enjoy every minute," even though our stress levels are off the charts.

If you're not feeling blissful, you are not alone. Parenting is much harder than we could have expected. Despite the picture painted by social media, *everyone* struggles. It's okay for you to love your kids and not love parenting.

But there is hope. There are ways for you to turn around your misery-to-joy ratio. You can have less fear, instability, and yelling, and more ease and cooperation. If you're at a low point, that's okay—the breakdown often comes before the breakthrough. My own feelings of shame and frustration broke me down; I was literally on the floor in tears, miserable. My breakthrough came when I gave up my idealistic expectations and started to focus on the place where I actually had some control: myself.

> If you do not know how to take care of yourself, and the violence in you, then you will not be able to take care of others. You must have love and patience before you can truly listen to your partner or child. If you are irritated you cannot listen. You have to know how to breathe mindfully, embrace your irritation and transform it. This is the true practice of love. —Thích Nhất Hạnh

About the Term "Parent"

The terms "parent" and "family" cover a wide range of relationships. Kids may be raised by grandparents, aunts and uncles, siblings, foster families, and other caregivers. If you are a caregiver for a child, good for you for reading this book and devoting your time, attention, and love to raising this young person! We don't yet have a single term that encompasses all of these, so for ease of reading, I use the term "parent" for all the caregivers involved in a child's life.

1

I Can't Control My Kids

They say it takes a village. Where can I get directions to this village? —Unknown

At some point, every reasonably alert parent realizes that they are not actually *in control* of their child. By the age of two, children clearly have their own minds and make their own choices. Yes, we can set expectations and standards—we can guide and coach our children—but they are not puppets on strings to be controlled.

After breaking down with the shame of yelling at my adorable toddler, I realized two things: (1) I didn't control *her*, and (2) I didn't actually have a whole lot of control over *myself* at that point. I didn't want to shout and scare my daughter. I had not consciously chosen to act like an enraged rhino, yet that's how I had behaved. It was time to focus my attention less on controlling my daughter's behavior and more on regulating myself. Letting my reactivity run the show wasn't working. It was actually leading to the very behaviors in my daughter that I wanted to avoid! It was *my* job to calm down.

Human emotions are highly contagious. You don't need to be around a grumpy teenager or euphoric toddler for long to become infected. Our moods, intentions, emotions, words, and actions clearly affect each other. So when a child feels upset, we start to feel upset. That's natural. When siblings shout at each other, when a toddler loses it (because you've given him the wrong color cup), we *feel* it. This makes parenting an emotional minefield. Yelling, crying, and whining naturally grate on our nervous system (more about this later). Our unconscious reaction is to make it stop! So we yell at our kids to calm down.

Yet parents are effectively telling children, "*You* change your behavior and emotions so that *I* can feel better." We're asking our children to regulate *our* feelings. However, we are the adults in the relationship—the ones with the fully developed brain and nervous system. Isn't it strange that we're asking our kids to calm down *when we can't*? Parenting is a relationship in which we, as adults, have the power and influence to change the dynamic.

Our locus of control really includes *only* ourselves. We can't control our kids' words and behaviors. We can't control how we were raised or what kind of genetic inheritance we were given. What *can* we control? At best, our own words and behaviors, from moment to moment. That requires us to be able to regulate ourselves. Hal Runkel, the author of *ScreamFree Parenting*, says it bluntly: "If you're not under control, you can't be in charge…To be in charge means controlling yourself so you can influence your kids."

Telling our kids to stop their upset feelings simply doesn't work. If we can regulate our emotions instead, we can be the calm mountain and give our children a solid anchor in their emotional storm. When we practice losing it less, we can respond more kindly and thoughtfully—providing the positive *influence* our children need.

I'm going to offer you a tool to help regulate your emotions in tough moments like these. But before we go any further, let's talk about practices in books. Most people will read the following exercise and keep on reading, not actually *doing* it. But not you, my friend. You know that no one gets better at tennis without time on the court. Concert violinists don't just hope they remember the notes, and NBA players don't just read about the game. Without some skin in the game, without giving these practices some time and effort, you'll soon forget everything you learn in this book. So let's agree that you are *not* the read-through-and-forget-it peruser; you are the let's-get-down-to-business-and-make-change kind of reader.

Here's a great in-the-moment tool that every parent needs to be the calm mountain in those challenging parenting moments. You can start immediately to shift your experience. As you downregulate, you'll be able to *be* the calm in the storm and respond to every situation more thoughtfully.

Tactical Breathing

Navy SEALs recognize that they do not make effective decisions when they're dysregulated, so calming down their stress response is a big priority. When a SEAL is in a stressful combat situation, they use *tactical breathing*, a super-simple way to slow down the heart rate and become more regulated:

1. Breathe in through the nostrils for a count of four.
2. Breathe out through the nostrils for a count of four.
3. Repeat four to six times.

If the four-count is difficult, reduce it to three. If it's too easy, increase it to five or six.

Take action: Are you expecting your child to calm down when you can't? If so, start to notice this pattern and instead turn your attention to yourself. Try tactical breathing to soothe your own upset feelings and model healthy emotional regulation.

2

I Just Want to Get It Right

Have no fear of perfection—you'll never reach it.
—Salvador Dalí

If you're anything like me, you want to be the new and improved, ideal parent—*now*, please! But growth doesn't work that way. My temper didn't transform all at once, and I made lots of mistakes in the learning process. Deep, lasting change takes time; meanwhile, we are still perfectly imperfect, mistake-making humans. You can expect a notable lag time between knowing what you want to do and actually being able to do it. And none of us will ever reach perfection. It doesn't exist in parenting. The very best you can aim for is "good enough."

The term "good enough mother" was first coined in 1953 by Donald Winnicott, a British pediatrician and psychoanalyst. He observed thousands of babies and their mothers, and he came to realize that babies and children actually *benefit* when their caretaker doesn't meet their every need.

This may seem counterintuitive, because for infants, it's best to meet their needs right away—as soon as the baby cries, we feed them or snuggle them or change their diaper. This kind of sensitive, attuned caregiving teaches our babies that they are safe and supports their feelings of security. However, we can't sustain this level of attentiveness to our children forever, nor should we. That is precisely what Winnicott shows us.

He believed that the way to be a good parent is to be a *good enough* parent. Children actually need their primary caretaker to "fail" them in tolerable ways regularly so they can learn to live in an imperfect world.

What does this look like? Winnicott didn't mean big failures like abuse and neglect. However, we parents live our lives and inevitably don't notice every bid for attention. We may not hear them calling right away. We may make a dinner they don't like. We make children do things they don't want to, like get in the car, stop playing, brush their teeth, or go to bed. All of these disappointments get our children ready to function in a world that will disappoint them regularly. They learn in small ways every day that the world doesn't revolve around them, that their every request won't be met, and that their behavior impacts other people. They experience the fact that life can be challenging, that they will feel disappointed, and they will still be okay.

If our children never have these experiences, they won't be able to manage the inevitable challenges. They won't learn that it's okay to feel bored, annoyed, sad, or disappointed and that they'll get through it. Good enough parenting builds our children's resilience.

Besides, perfection is not an option. When we strive for perfection, we set ourselves up for disappointment, because holding "perfect" as the ideal means we are *never* good enough. Mistakes and imperfections are what make us human. So instead of perfection, can we offer ourselves a little grace? Can we allow our kids to be mistake-making humans too? Instead of perfection, let us practice instead to be *present*—to really be here for both the good and the bad. When we can be present for the uncomfortable things, we're more able to be present for the joy life brings, and we can offer our kids truly unconditional love.

Striving for perfection means being attached to a certain outcome. We're seeking this thing that is outside of us, separate from us. We're seeking to control, and we're constantly afraid of not being good enough. We become attached to our children's being a certain way. These expectations make our love conditional, so that our children feel that *Mom or Dad loves me only if...*

Giving ourselves (and our kids) permission to be human—permission to be good enough—frees us to be wholly ourselves. We're allowed to be enough even when we make the inevitable mistakes. When our children see us do that for ourselves—when we model presence over perfection—time after time, they absorb a deep sense of compassion for themselves and for others.

Take action: Are you striving for unrealistic perfection? If so, why? Journal on the drive for perfection and how it affects your life. What would giving yourself permission to be human feel like?

3

Eek! My Child Sounds Just Like Me

Parenting is theater. We're showing, not telling our children... —Stan Tatkin

When my second-born daughter was around one year old, she started to toddle around and would inevitably mess up her sister's toys. One day, hearing a problem arising, I walked over to the sunroom just in time to see my older daughter harshly barking orders to her sister, who sat amid a pile of ruined block towers. Big sister was saying things like, "Don't touch that! Put that down!"

It was a moment of awakening for me. Oh. That's what I sound like. I felt like a mirror was shining right back on me. Although I was encouraging my older daughter to use kind words with her sister, she was doing what I do, not what I'd explicitly taught.

Kids are often not great at doing what we tell them to do, but they are wonderful imitators. They are attuned to our behaviors and watch us every day. We are their model, and our behavior creates a pattern that our children may follow for a lifetime. Does this make you squirm a little? It did for me.

The onus is on us to behave the way we want our children to behave. The onus was on me to change the way I spoke to my daughters.

This meant shouting "Be quiet!" wouldn't cut it. Instead, I needed to model lowering my voice (whispering to your child works wonders). It turns out that when *we're* mad, it's completely ineffective to order *them* to calm down. When family members are upset, it's *our* job—as the grown-ups in this situation (the ones with a fully developed brain)—to downregulate our nervous system. We have to model calming down. We can't expect our child to do something that we can't.

We often feel frustrated when our child doesn't want to apologize for something they did or said. We feel we must *make* them apologize. Yet there is a far simpler answer: When you make mistakes, apologize to your child—model the behavior you want to see. We may worry that we're not "strong" or "respected" if we apologize. Not so. It's safe and healthy for you to model being perfectly imperfect and making amends. You teach your child the true strength of self-acceptance instead of defensiveness.

Your children will pick up whatever you practice in your lifestyle and habits—the kinds of food you eat, whether you eat together as a family, your media consumption habits, your relationship with your phone, and more. Do you want your child to do what you are doing? To say what you are saying? The power of your influence is far greater than the impact of anything you directly say to your child. It's daunting—but consider it an *opportunity*. Anything you change in yourself is really a two-for-one deal: When you make positive changes for yourself, you model that for your child too.

Understanding the power of modeling is an opportunity to change generational patterns. You can make a positive impact not only for your immediate family but for generations beyond. We don't have to be perfect, but we can remember that our words matter, our habits matter, and our own healing matters quite a lot.

Take action: If you have a parenting partner, talk with them about what you want for your child. Are you modeling positive behaviors and communication? Are you living what you want your child to learn?

4

"I'm a Terrible Parent"

Most unhappy people need to learn just one lesson: how to see themselves through the lens of genuine compassion and treat themselves accordingly. —Martha Beck

There was a time when I was getting triggered and yelling at my little one—I'm embarrassed to say how often. You might say to yourself, *I'm losing my temper, I'm frustrated, and I'm modeling stress eating* (or whatever your personal struggle is). *I'm messing up my kids. I'm a terrible parent.* I understand this internal dialogue because I lived it. I told myself I was a terrible mother, that I was failing, and that I sucked at this job.

This kind of self-talk only left me in an ineffective puddle of pity on the floor. Berating myself made me feel stuck and totally incapacitated. The harsh inner voice didn't help me become a better parent to my child. It feels bad, and it doesn't even work! Yet this kind of self-talk is common.

This is a fundamental parenting problem that's often invisible. Physiologically, when we harshly criticize ourselves, we're tapping into the body's threat-defense system—the fight, flight, or freeze response. Feeling threatened puts stress on the mind and body, and long-term stress can cause anxiety and depression, which is why habitual self-criticism is so bad for emotional and physical well-being. With harsh self-criticism, we are both the attacker and the attacked. We are also not as likely to try something new, because our inevitable human mistakes lead to self-criticism/attack. All this self-judgment and criticism keeps us well and truly *stuck*.

Suffering, difficulty, and mistakes are part of the human experience. Confronting personal failings is an unavoidable part of being a parent, and that can be painful. There's another way to recognize the reality that it's hard right now. Ask yourself, *How can I comfort and care for myself in this moment?* This affects both you and your child because, remember, you're modeling in every moment.

It's far more practical to practice *self-compassion*—treating ourselves with kindness and understanding—than it is to be hard on ourselves. It may feel weird, but when we talk to ourselves as we would talk to a good friend, we're able to recover faster, pick ourselves up, and try again. It makes us feel cared for and more secure. We're able to downregulate our nervous system threat response. When we try something new and inevitably make a mistake, the soft landing of self-compassion helps us try again.

When we practice self-compassion, we tap into our innate nurturing system and naturally become more effective and responsive parents. As you develop more compassion for yourself, you'll have more compassion for your child and everyone around you.

Self-compassion has three components:

1. Mindfulness—being aware of your thoughts and feelings. What is the inner voice saying? You can't change what you're not aware of. So you observe your feelings without repressing or exaggerating them.

2. Self-kindness—recognizing that you are suffering in this moment and responding with care. You can talk to yourself as you would talk to a dear friend who feels this way.

3. Common humanity— you remind yourself that everyone makes mistakes. We all yell at our kids sometimes. Remind yourself that it isn't "just me" who messes up. It's part of being human.

You will have many opportunities to practice self-compassion. For parents, it's a game-changer, because children inevitably bring up your baggage. They seem to have an innate knack for zeroing in on things that drive us bananas. Here's a way to practice:

Self-Compassion Break

Self-compassion researcher Kristin Neff teaches this practice. Either bring to mind a difficult moment to practice, or use it when life's inevitable difficulty arrives:

1. Say to yourself, *This is a moment of suffering,* or *This hurts*. This is being mindfully aware of what's happening.

2. Next, say to yourself, *Suffering is part of life,* or *I'm not alone and we all struggle*. This is remembering our common humanity.

3. Finally, put a hand on your heart and say to yourself, *May I be kind to myself,* or *May I give myself the compassion that I need,* or any words you might say to a dear friend who feels as you do.

Self-compassion grows with practice. If you don't have a lot now, or if it feels awkward and strange to be kind to yourself, that's *okay*. What you practice grows stronger, so keep practicing.

Take action: Write down the three elements of self-compassion on a sticky note to remind yourself to practice. How would you talk to a good friend who felt this way?

5

I'm Losing It

Kids do idiotic, obnoxious stuff. That's unlikely to change any time soon, so if your plan for keeping your cool depends on your child's ability to do the same, that's going to end poorly for everyone. —Carla Naumburg

When I yelled at my daughter, I blamed myself. I believed that I had *chosen* to yell at my child, yet the last thing I wanted to do was lose my temper! No one wants to shout at their kids. No one *chooses* to lose it. We don't consciously plan to holler, so why are we blaming ourselves?

Think about this:

Yelling is not your fault, but it is your responsibility.

It's your job to take responsibility for your behavior and take steps to downregulate your emotional response. So how do you do that?

First, understand your reactivity. Imagine that your child is freaking out about putting on their shoes—whining, and throwing the shoes. You can feel your stress rising. Your nervous system is registering your child as a threat, just as your ancient ancestors might have reacted to a predator. Though there is no imminent danger, your nervous system prepares you to fight off a threat or flee to safety—by raising your heart rate, tightening your muscles, and so on.

This stress response bypasses the slower parts of your brain to react as quickly as possible. The trouble is, the parts of the brain that process more slowly are exactly the parts we need to respond effectively to our kids—namely, the prefrontal cortex, or PFC. Neuroscientists have shown that the PFC regulates attention, thought, and action (Goldman-Rakic, 1987). Moreover, it inhibits "inappropriate motor responses" (Aron, Robbins, and Poldrack 2004)—so if we want to avoid yelling, or to be able to choose a more thoughtful response, we really need the PFC to be online.

This hijacking of the PFC by your stress response is why most parenting advice doesn't take hold. When little Elliot throws the shoes, our nervous system feels threatened, and we can't even *access* the new parenting advice we've learned. All that well-meaning guidance flies out the window, and we're left feeling frustrated and blaming ourselves.

We can see that downregulating our own nervous system is parenting priority number one. We *have* to calm our reactivity in order to respond compassionately and effectively.

When people ask me "How do I stop yelling?," one of the first things I point them to is the overall amount of stress in their lives. If you have a lot of stress in your life, it doesn't take much to push you into losing it. Reducing stress can give you the space to use your whole brain.

To be a good parent, you must take care of yourself. This means getting enough sleep, regular exercise, and time with friends and family. Exercise provides stress relief and helps your body release endorphins, which increase your feelings of overall well-being. Lack of sleep can negatively impact everything you do, as well as every relationship. Finally, social support can create a buffer against stress, keeping you healthier and happier. Friends can pick you up when you're sad, provide insights when you're confused, and help you have fun when you need to blow off steam.

I know: Reducing your overall stress is a *big* ask! You may be personally struggling with multiple challenges for which you need support. Here in the US, most parents are radically undersupported by the structure of our society, leading them to feel overwhelmed. If your circumstances are adding layers of stress to your life, it may not be your fault. I would love to see a world where parents have more support and a greater sense of safety so we can give our best to our children.

Reducing your overall stress and reactivity will take time. I encourage you to take any steps you can to bring more ease into your life.

What can we do to reduce our reactivity in the midst of a difficult moment? Deep breathing is cliché because it works, so I'm going to share a method here. This breath moves the body out of fight-or-flight into the parasympathetic, rest-and-relax response. You can use it to calm down, to go to sleep, or whenever you notice tension in your body. Write this technique on sticky notes and place strategic reminders all around your house:

4-7-8 Breathing

Since the fight, flight, or freeze response impairs our parenting, we need to engage the opposite, "rest and relax" or parasympathetic nervous system response, to have access to the whole brain. 4-7-8 breathing is a technique for deep relaxation conceived by Harvard-trained medical doctor and founder of the Arizona Center for Integrative Medicine Dr. Andrew Weil. It doesn't matter how fast you do this breathing; the important part is keeping the exhale longer than the inhale.

Here's how you do it:

1. Breathe in through your nose for a count of four.
2. Hold your breath for a count of seven (skip or shorten the hold if it makes you anxious).
3. Exhale through your mouth for a count of eight. Feel free to make an audible "whoosh" sound.
4. Repeat four times.

Take action: Try 4-7-8 breathing at key points in your day, like when you wake up, after getting home from work, and before transitions (like bedtime) with your child.

6

How Can I Help My Child Chill?

The capacity for self-soothing is born out of hundreds and hundreds of instances of being soothed by someone else.
—Rachel Samson

When my daughter was a toddler, like many parents I directed her actions nearly all the time. I ordered her around constantly! "Put your shoes on." "Take your shoes off." "Come over here. Don't go there." And so on. Being the highly sensitive kid that she is, all of this unskillful parenting set her off, and she pushed back. I'd double down, raising my voice. Then she would get more upset, yelling, and I would get more upset. She would lose it, and then I would lose it. It was a mess.

I was desperate for her to calm down so that I could feel better. I wish I'd understood then that many of her "difficult" behaviors and "not listening" probably arose from her stress response. I also wish I'd known that I had to calm down so that she could.

Kids have the same fight, flight, or freeze stress response that we do. Just as our nervous system can register our kid's behavior as a threat, our child's stress response can be triggered by us parents. We are bigger, louder, and stronger than small children, and when we stand and yell, it feels really threatening to a child's nervous system. The behavior we see as "bad" is often driven by the fight, flight, or freeze response.

What does this look like? *Fight* can look like kicking, screaming, spitting, pushing, throwing things, clenched fists, glaring, or even gasping for breath. *Flight* can look like darting eyes, restlessness, excessive fidgeting, doing anything to get away, and running. *Freeze* can look like holding breath, shutting down, feeling unable to move, escaping into their own mind, and feeling numb.

Traditional Western parenting tactics like yelling, ordering, and threatening can trigger our kids' stress response, causing them to lose access to their (still not fully developed) PFC and therefore become unable to learn anything we want to teach them in that moment. When we understand the biology of a child's nervous system, we can see that these tactics are simply ineffective.

So what do we do? For better or worse, my child was highly attuned to my feelings, and when I got upset, it only made things worse. We were highly intertwined, and she depended on me to help her regulate her feelings. Again, the first priority must always be our own emotional regulation, because (1) we don't want to escalate the situation by setting off our kid's stress response, (2) the best way to teach kids how to calm down is through modeling, and (3) kids *coregulate* their emotions *with* us.

The holy grail of parenting is our children becoming able to regulate their emotions. When they can calm themselves down (*hallelujah!*), much of the chaos of early childhood calms down too. But before children can regulate their own feelings, they first learn to regulate with others, *then* they gradually learn to use these regulation tools more independently. This starts with us becoming attuned to our child's emotional state in infancy and soothing any upset feelings. Coregulation is when caregivers support kids emotionally so they can develop their own self-regulation.

We can teach kids to regulate their emotions through regulating our own feelings (creating an emotionally safe environment) and coaching them on how to regulate their feelings. Here's how:

1. **Label your own and your child's feelings out loud.** We "name it to tame it." Acknowledging difficult feelings out loud teaches healthy emotional intelligence and helps us get to the next steps.

2. **Model calming down.** Say, "I'm feeling upset, and I'm going to breathe/take a break/and so on to calm down." Use 4-7-8 breathing and other tools you'll find in this book.

3. **Attune to and listen to your child's feelings.** When your child is sharing their thoughts and feelings with you, practice giving them your undivided attention. Validate—reflect back—your understanding without judgment.

4. **Help your child soothe or problem solve.** *After* acknowledging the feelings and downregulating the emotions, it's time to coach your child on skillful ways to handle the situation.

We can help our kids calm down by creating a home environment that supports learning about how to take care of our feelings.

Create a Calm-Down Kit

A calm-down kit is simply a collection of objects and items that help children cope with their emotions, positively and safely. Gather the items, place them in a backpack or cloth bag, and take the kit with you in your car or on the go. You can use the calm-down kit during downtime too, to practice and figure out which items help in times of distress. Some ideas:

- Cards/printouts with calming ideas
- Books about emotions
- Small photo album of loved ones
- A special blanket
- Stuffed animal
- Soothing music and headphones
- Blank notebook and crayons, pencils, markers, or similar
- Pinwheels, to encourage deep breathing and blowing out
- Coloring books
- Play-Doh
- Emotions poster

Take action: Create your own calm-down kit with the help of your child this week. Talk about emotions and teach your child about their stress response.

7

The Stress Is Getting to Me

Mindfulness is a way of befriending ourselves and our experience. —Jon Kabat-Zinn

Just like my daughter, I was an intense, highly sensitive kid. For as long as I can remember, I've felt *too* much—I was on an emotional roller-coaster. When I was up, life felt exuberant, but when I was down, I lived in a pit of despair. These pits came regularly—every week or two I felt overwhelmed by life. This roller-coaster was exhausting and led me to start to learn about mindfulness. I wanted the freedom of equanimity (cue angelic singing).

Mindfulness teachers from the Buddhist tradition promised that more clarity, ease, and wisdom was attainable—that we *all* have the possibility of transcending our suffering. In fact, when asked about his teaching, the Buddha himself said, "I teach suffering and the cessation of suffering" (Bodhi 2013). That's what I wanted, so I started doing a lot of reading.

I read books about mindfulness for about a decade before I actually sat down for a meditation session. After doing yoga teacher training, I finally realized that I could do it, and I started practicing regularly: ten minutes a day, six days a week. I set a timer and attempted to bring my attention back to my breath. It wasn't fun. A few months in, after a frustrating session, I thought, *This isn't working! I'm just sitting here thinking the whole time!* Then I reflected on the rest of my life, and I realized something big, something life-changing had happened: *I had not fallen into any of my pits!* Mindfulness meditation truly transformed my life. Rather than being subsumed by the waves, I was finally learning to surf.

Around the same time, I started to see mindfulness in the news a lot. Modern scientists were confirming many of the benefits of mindfulness touted by ancient wisdom. Nowadays we have a plethora of scientific evidence about the positive benefits of mindfulness meditation, from the quality of our sleep to how well we cope with and recover from illness (Rusch et al. 2018). Researchers from Johns Hopkins University found forty-seven studies showing that mindfulness meditation helps ease anxiety, depression, and chronic pain (Goyal). It also increases *positive* emotion (Davidson et al. 2002). It seems that mindfulness actually *does* decrease our suffering.

When I became a parent, I turned back to mindfulness to help me cope. I was particularly interested in research showing how mindfulness practices can increase social connection and emotional intelligence and, importantly, improve your ability to regulate your emotions (Fredrickson et al. 2008). *Improve your ability to regulate your emotions*—this is just what I yearned for! I needed to be able to access my whole brain so I could choose how to respond. Mindfulness was coming to the rescue again. All in a free practice that helps me feel clearer, calmer, and happier, with no harmful side-effects.

I started to see mindfulness everywhere. Besides the explosion of research, people like famous basketball coach Phil Jackson were embracing mindfulness. Jackson had the Chicago Bulls and the

L.A. Lakers learn meditation as a way to improve their focus and teamwork. He found that mindfulness helped the players pay attention to what was happening on the court moment to moment. This has paid off—Jackson has led more teams to championships than any other coach in the NBA.

CEOs started practicing meditation to give themselves the extra attentional edge for success. Therapists embraced mindfulness practices, realizing that meditation can help their clients positively alter their reactions to daily experience. Public schools started teaching mindfulness practices to help students reduce the negative effects of stress and increase their ability to stay engaged. The US Department of Defense now teaches mindfulness in the military to help soldiers perform at their best and reduce pain and stress related to post-deployment and post-traumatic stress disorder (PTSD).

Mindfulness meditation does *not* make us perfect. It doesn't make it so we never have difficult feelings anymore. We'll still make mistakes, and we will definitely still mess up sometimes. However, mindfulness meditation does strengthen the qualities that psychologists say are crucial to happiness: resilience, equanimity, calm, and a sense of compassionate connection to others. Science has shown what meditators have known for a long time: meditation helps us be calmer and happier.

The science and stories that have come from this explosion in mindfulness are heartening because a large new group of people now feel comfortable taking advantage of meditation's many benefits. If deployed soldiers, children, NBA players, and people in high-stress occupations like surgery can use mindfulness to their advantage, why not parents?

Take action: What benefits of mindfulness would you like to strengthen in your own life? How would this help you? What ripple effects might there be?

8

Why Am I Not Enjoying Parenting?

The bad stuff is easier to believe. You ever notice that?
—Julia Roberts' character, Vivian, in *Pretty Woman*

Before I was a meditator, I used to get really frustrated with myself. While I wanted to be a positive person, my head would often be filled with complaints and general grumbling about the world. I would ruminate for days on a mistake I'd made. *What's wrong with me?* I wondered. Positive thinking books told me that if I wanted to change myself, I should change my thoughts, but the pessimistic thoughts kept coming. My default outlook on life was running me down.

I was far from alone in my gloom. This *negativity bias* is a tendency that all humans share. It's not even our fault: blame our forebears. Our ancestors who lived to pass down their genes were the ones who got better and better at looking out for threats and danger. Imagine you're an ancient human: as you move about the world, you may find a wild strawberry patch and note where that is, but it's *more* important to be wary of signs of dangerous predators (so you don't get eaten). The happy-go-lucky ancients who didn't worry about saber-toothed tigers were not as likely to pass along their genes. The ones who survived passed down an innate bias toward seeing problems, threats, and danger. This is the negativity bias—the fact that the brain, to help us survive, preferentially looks for, reacts to, stores, and then recalls negative information over positive information.

Psychologist Rick Hanson summed up the human mind's propensity: "The mind is like Velcro for negative experiences, and Teflon for positive ones." We naturally give more attention to difficulties and bad news. Yikes.

Our human default settings do *not* help us be relaxed, content, and therefore able to be understanding and in tune with our child. Our minds and bodies, optimized for survival, are wired to look out for problems, leaving us anxious, stressed, and unable to parent well. Connection is the glue that makes parenting easier, and the negativity bias can actively undermine it. Our view of our children can become narrow and biased. We see the *un*cooperative moments rather than the cooperative ones. We see their selfish moments but miss their generosity.

On top of our negativity bias and our stress response, we now know that trauma and stress can be passed down from one generation to the next. Scientists have found that genetic impacts from things like smoking, a stressed childhood, famine, and other traumas can be passed down from generation to generation. One study found that Holocaust survivors' children, who were more likely to have stress disorders, had gene changes that could *only* be attributed to Holocaust exposure in their parents (Yehuda et al. 2015). Knowing that many human societies had some very cruel, violent practices in the past, we can see how many of us may carry the genetic effects of trauma.

Our default human settings include (1) a nervous system wired to react to threats, (2) innate negativity bias, and (3) possibly genetically passed-on trauma. Without any effort to oppose these defaults, we try to keep stress at bay, but anxiety keeps us awake at night. We want to be present with our kids, but our thoughts are continually jumping to the past or future. We focus on what's wrong with them and with ourselves. We're on autopilot, going in a million different directions. Plus, as we live more technologically connected lives, we're frequently distracted. We may not be aware that stress creeps in; then suddenly we're losing it with our kids—and feeling guilty.

These are not all new human problems. Thousands of years ago, the Buddha observed that life always involves suffering and that even when things seem good, we always feel an undercurrent of anxiety and uncertainty inside. I believe he was an astute observer of our default tendencies.

Are we doomed to be miserable? No. This can be changed—we can actually use our mind to shift our brain to change our mind. We can use the brain's natural plasticity to literally reshape it and change our nervous systems. (More on this soon.)

It may seem like a load of bad news to read about our innate human default setting, but I invite you to consider how it's helpful. Ignorance is *not* bliss. When we are unconscious of the habits and tendencies that drive us, we are completely at their mercy. You have no perspective on your mind or behavior; the defaults are running the show. As soon as you can start to see this—as soon as you *notice* this—you have perspective. Instead of *being* the tendency, you are the *observer* of it. This is the powerful beginning of mindful change.

Take action: Observe yourself this week to see if you can notice when your mind veers toward the negative—seeing the "bad" behavior. Try to shift your focus to what your child does that is kind, generous, helpful, or generally positive.

9

On the Road to Calm

Between stimulus and response there is space. In that space is our power to choose our response. In our response lies our growth and our freedom. —Victor Frankl

Through my default tendencies, I practiced anxiousness, distractibility, emotional lows, and stress for *years*—with all that practice, I became really good at these conditions. But research shows that new experiences literally reshape the brain, and with my relationship with my daughter on the line, I couldn't wait to practice mindfulness.

Mindfulness is a state of being, and meditation is the classic way we practice. Mindfulness is the practice of bringing our attention to the present moment, with an attitude of kindness and curiosity. Mindfulness is a type of awareness where we purposefully guide our attention to the sounds, feelings, and sense experiences that happen to be here and now, without judging what we find, and with an open heart. It's a practice of being aware of our thoughts—and not getting carried away by them. It's about being *present*—in tune with our body, our senses, and the elements around us, moment to moment. In Chinese, the ideogram for mindfulness is the character for "presence" or "now" above the character for "heart." So we can think of mindfulness as *present heart*.

Contrary to its image in pop culture, meditation does *not* involve sitting cross-legged on a cloud, basking in transcendent bliss, with rainbow sparkles shooting out your ears. Meditation is ridiculously simple and easy. Try it right now in three steps:

1. Sit comfortably. Close your eyes if you want to.
2. Bring your full attention to a neutral sensation in the present moment, like the feeling of your breath coming in and out, or the feeling of your hands touching your legs.
3. You will be distracted by any number of things—*What should we have for dinner? Why is* Stairway to Heaven *such a long song? Why do we write* donut *instead of* doughnut? *Am I doing this right? I don't think I'm doing this right.* This is normal and not a problem. Just notice that you're distracted, and start again.

Meditation is all about step 3. That moment when we notice we are totally lost in thought is actually a golden moment in meditation. It's meditation's bicep curl, as you are actually strengthening your attention, focus, clarity, and calm. The goal of meditation is *not* to clear your mind, but to bring your mind back to the present moment, again and again (and again and again). The present moment sensation you choose to return to—the feeling of breathing or touch—is your *anchor*, keeping your ship from going off course.

This is hard at first, so I encourage you to start small, with five minutes or even less.

Meditation is fundamentally a simple practice: a gym session for the mind. As we practice returning attention to the present moment whenever we notice that we're distracted, we see how our mind ziplines from thoughts to ideas to judgments to planning. Feelings and impulses arise out of nowhere. We feel fidgety. We start to see our issues. (That the voice in our head can be incredibly judgy!) And we start to feel like we suck at this meditation thing.

Don't give up! Just continue to bring your attention back to your anchor. As you sit regularly, over time you'll become aware of previously unconscious mental habits. Unconscious habits can rule you, driving your thoughts and actions automatically. But when you start to notice them, you interrupt the mental pattern, and *then* you can start to change. As you practice observing your mind's chaos—feeling impulses, but *not* reacting—you can start to see thoughts as just that: words or images that exist only in your head. You start to see how useless your judgments are. Bit by bit, you become calmer and less reactive—not necessarily while meditating, but in your active life.

MRI brain scans of meditators show that these changes aren't just perceived, but are physical changes in the brain structure. After an eight-week course of mindfulness meditation practice, the brain's fight-or-flight response centers, the amygdalae, actually appear to shrink. And as the amygdalae shrink, the PFC (associated with awareness, empathy, and decision making) actually becomes thicker! The functional connectivity between these regions—how often they are activated together—also changes. The connections between the fight-or-flight centers and the rest of the brain weakens, while the connections among areas associated with *attention* get stronger. Meditation literally changes the brain in a way that weakens our reactivity.

I've seen how a regular mindfulness meditation practice creates more calm, peace, and groundedness in parents. It's like a medicine with no side effects that steadies the heart, the mind, and the nervous system. A mindfulness practice allows us to really be present, rather than distracted on autopilot, which may be the best motivator to practice.

Take action: Try the three-step meditation practice in this chapter. What do you notice? Can you set a timer for sixty seconds and see what happens?

10

Mindfulness for Busy Parents

Mindfulness isn't difficult, we just need to remember to do it.
—Sharon Salzberg

When you meditate, you introduce far-reaching and long-lasting benefits into your life. You can lower your stress and reactivity, improve your focus and your connections to others, and reduce brain chatter. So how do you do it?

I read books about mindfulness for a decade before I started practicing. A *decade*! Through that experience, I found out that (lo and behold) *application* of something makes a far greater impact than reading about it. Just as reading about tennis will not make you a better player than time on the court will, dear reader, you will get far more out of this if you actually *practice* mindfulness. In this chapter, I'm going to share some of my favorite and most practical ways for busy parents to actually reap some of the benefits of mindfulness. Even if you have an infant or can't sit still.

First, the gold standard of mindfulness practice: sitting meditation. No, you don't have to contort your legs or hold your hands in a funny way. In fact, you can practice sitting meditation anywhere you sit! Got a La-Z-Boy? Go for it. As long as you can be comfortable *and* alert, it counts.

Sitting Meditation

Sitting meditation is about bringing your attention back to the present moment with an attitude of curiosity and kindness. We develop the ability to be comfortable in our own skin.

To start a sitting meditation practice:

- Find a place and time to sit where you can be (relatively) undistracted. If you have a parenting partner, you may have to ask for help with this.
- Sit in a position that's comfortable for you, that you can stay in for a while. (You want to stay awake, so maybe not *too* comfortable.)
- Start small, three to five minutes at a time for the first week. *Even one minute of mindfulness meditation a day is better than none at all.* Work your way up to fifteen minutes (maybe a few years later).
- Aim to practice six days a week at about the same time each day.
- Begin with guided meditation. It helps to have a teacher reminding you what you're doing! (See the free tools at https://www.mindfulmamamentor.com/bookbonus.)
- Unclench your jaw and let your belly be soft. You don't have to fight your way through your meditation experience.

- Choose a neutral sensation in the present moment as your anchor to bring yourself back when your mind wanders. This can be the breath, the feeling of sitting, or ambient sounds.
- Your goal is to relax and gently bring your attention back to your anchor without judgment.
- Don't expect blissful clarity and angelic singing. Bring your curiosity and kindness to whatever you experience.
- When you notice your mind wandering, it can help to *note* it. You may say to yourself silently *thinking, planning*, and so on.
- End each session with kindness. Congratulate yourself for doing the practice!
- At first, reward yourself for your practice time—this will help you to build and ingrain this life-transforming new habit. Eventually your new equanimity will be all the reward you need to keep it up.

Calm, Peace Meditation

When your mind is going bonkers during meditation, it helps to have something more than the breath to return you to the present moment. In Thích Nhất Hạnh's Plum Village community, they teach rhyming phrases that can act as an anchor. Do this meditation in the same manner as the sitting meditation above, but repeat these phrases silently in conjunction with your breathing:

1. *Breathing in, I calm my body. Breathing out, I feel peace.*
2. *Breathing in, I smile, Breathing out, I release.*
3. As the phrases become more familiar, you can shorten to *Calm, peace, smile, release.*

These practices are a fantastic basic toolkit for mindfulness meditation. You can use them interchangeably; each will help you steady your heart, mind, and nervous system, helping you become a calmer, more grounded parent.

Take action: Pick a time of day to start a short meditation practice. Put it in your calendar and set a reminder. Then head over to the free tools at https://www.mindfulmamamentor.com/bookbonus to get the guided meditations, and practice!

11

Mindfulness for Fidgety Parents

The mind can go in a thousand directions, but on this beautiful path, I walk in peace. With each step, the wind blows. With each step, a flower blooms.

—Thích Nhất Hạnh

If when you read "meditation" you think, "I'm outta here," I get it. I have a lot of anxious energy that I need to burn off, so for many years sitting still sounded like a form of torture. But I'm here to tell you that *you will survive* the effort. However, if you have a lot of fidgety, anxious energy, try easing into mindfulness practices with *moving* meditations.

If you hate to sit still, walking meditation is a simple and totally legit way to practice meditation that you can easily fit into your life. Walking meditation is about slowing down, feeling each footstep, and breathing peacefully.

My daughter was in preschool at a Montessori center just a short distance from my house. I used to drop her off and dash home—literally running back so I could efficiently use those few short hours she was in school. Until I realized that my rushing was actually *increasing* my anxiety and stress. So I started practicing mindful walking instead of running. The results were startling: Not only was I more relaxed, but I got more done! My relaxed mind and body could think more clearly and thus act with greater intention and efficiency. I was also happier when I came to pick her up. Win-win!

Mindful walking—walking with the intention to bring our attention and senses to the present moment—is a great way to be present with our children. Small children are naturally in the present moment, alert and curious about the world around them. When we practice mindful walking, instead of rushing our kids from place to place, we can join them in appreciating the beauty here and now: vegetation poking up through the cracks, the feeling of our child's hand in ours.

Walking meditation is a way to stop our frantic running into the future and appreciate the moment. Regardless of how restless you may be, walking meditation can channel your energy into calm and give you all the benefits of a sitting mindfulness practice. Here's how to do it:

Walking Meditation

1. **Choose a place to walk**. Your goal is to bring your attention back to the present moment with kindness and curiosity—not to actually get somewhere. So walking meditation can be done back and forth in a room, up and down a street, or circularly, like on a track.

2. **Set a timer.** You can set a timer for five or ten minutes or set a distance, as I did with the walk home from school.

3. **Walk with intention.** We're so used to walking to get somewhere that it may feel a little weird to just walk with the intention of being present. That's okay. Relax and appreciate the present moment.

4. **Focus your attention.** Bring your attention to the feeling of raising each foot and setting it down, the feeling of your feet on the earth. What are you aware of in the present moment? Connect with your senses. If you're outside, feel the air on your skin: Is it damp or dry?

5. **Notice when your mind wanders.** You will probably start thinking about things to do later, start a list in your head, or decide what you should have said in an earlier interaction with your child. This is totally

normal! Whenever you realize that you're lost in thought, notice how it makes it more difficult to connect to your senses. Then gently, kindly return your attention to the feeling of your feet on the ground.

6. **Pause**. Stop for a moment and take in your surroundings with all of your senses.
7. **Resist the habit of speeding up or running.** Even if it feels strange, practice slowing down.
8. **Try a helpful phrase.** I like to coordinate this phrase with the rhythm of my breathing (another Plum Village practice): *I have arrived. I am home. In the here, and the now.*
9. **Congratulate yourself for practicing**. Celebrate: Doing a walking meditation practice is definitely a win!

Take action: Today or tomorrow, take a few minutes to try walking meditation, even if just briefly. Try it walking back to your car after an errand or even back and forth in your home. Notice how it feels.

12

I Want to Be There for These Moments

Just because our eyes are open does not mean we are awake. —Haemin Sunim

Picture this: You are walking to the park with your child in early spring warmth. You feel the fresh breeze on your bare arms. You see the crocuses popping up. You feel the softness of the ground, moisture in the air, the sun on your face. Your body is relaxed. Your child puts her hand in yours, soft and warm against your cooler skin. Then she slips her hand away to run off and inspect a worm. You are present and able to enjoy this day. Nothing special is happening, but you are awake to the life that is here.

Now take the same setting, but this time you are preoccupied with your thoughts. Items on your to-do list pop to mind. You're worried that you're missing something. You start thinking about your older son and his difficulties at school. Your daughter tugs at your hand to go look at a worm. "No," you say, "we have to get going." You take out your phone to see if there are emails since your walk began. You tug your daughter's hand as you walk away.

In this second scenario, you are barely aware of your surroundings, caught up in your ruminating thoughts. You don't really notice your body, but if you did, you'd find that it is tense and constricted, like your mind. Your relationship with your child has narrowed down to getting her from here to there, another to-do.

Even though these situations look the same to the casual observer, we can see that when we're distracted, we miss the life that's right here. We miss our chance to witness our child experiencing her world. We are not present for our life.

It's easy to fall into these patterns. Our mind's default settings are to scan for threats, so without conscious effort to change this, we're distracted for much of our lives. This is why the mindfulness practices are so important: so we can actually be there for our children. The present moment is *the only place* where we can connect with loved ones.

You can build a present-moment muscle over time. Imagine our walking-to-the-park scenario: As you leave the house, *set an intention* to be aware of your surroundings and your child. Practice to appreciate your environment and the sensation of walking. You will become distracted—when you notice this, label it in your mind: *thinking*. Remember that *simply noticing is a win*. When you notice your distraction, celebrate it! Then return your attention to the present moment.

Mindfulness is not something that we learn once and we're done. It takes conscious practice and a lot of patience. You are building the attention muscle that is quite weak for most of us.

Practicing being present is the key to everything important in parenting. We want our children to be securely attached—to be resilient, confident, able to regulate their emotions and have positive relationships. Journalist Bethany Saltman investigated attachment for more than a decade for her book, *Strange Situation* (2020), and found that "what the attachment research makes clear is that it's the capacity for self-awareness of even our so-called failures that leads to self-compassion, which leads to a more relaxed attachment system, which leads to mutual delight, which leads to a secure pattern of attachment."

Dr. Daniel Siegel, clinical professor of psychiatry, author, and expert on attachment, mindfulness, and the brain, agrees: "parental presence is key to optimizing the chance of your child having a life of well-being and resilience" (Clarke-Fields 2018). Becoming more present matters.

You can practice presence *with* your children. Here's a practice that will strengthen your mindfulness muscle and give your child the one thing they crave most: your *attention*.

Mindful Special Time

Special time is time that you set aside regularly to spend playing one-on-one with your child. Your child picks and leads the activity; you follow along with your undivided attention. Here's how:

1. Give it a name ("special time" or "[your child's name] and Mom/Dad time").
2. Let your child know when it's special time. Set a timer for five, ten, or fifteen minutes.
3. Allow your child to pick the activity—anything besides screen time. You can preselect a few toys if needed.
4. Practice being 100-percent present during special time. Put away all distractions, like phones, work, and other electronics. Put the spotlight of your attention on your child with an attitude of kindness and curiosity. Your mind will wander—that's normal. Just keep bringing your attention back to your child—your child is the anchor for your attention.
5. Follow your child's lead—do what they do, and say what they say. During these few minutes, don't place any demands on your child, such as asking questions or giving instructions.
6. Have fun!
7. End special time by telling your child what you appreciate about that time.
8. Step away and allow your child to continue playing, if possible.

This practice is a powerful win-win in so many ways. You're not only practicing mindful awareness, with all of its benefits, but also strengthening your child's attachment and relationship with you. Committing to just five or ten minutes of mindful special time with your child regularly will help you become more present and help your child feel secure and become calmer and more cooperative.

Take action: Announce to your child that you are going to have special time today. Explain how it will work, then try it out!

13

Story Time

The mind is its own place and, in itself can make a heaven of hell or a hell of heaven. —John Milton

When I scared my adorable toddler, I knew I was a "terrible mother"—or at least that's what the voice in my head said. *What did I think I was doing having kids?* I berated myself for my failure. These thoughts left me utterly incapacitated—I became a pathetic wreck, curled up in a ball, crying.

To move on from that hellish moment, I had to tell myself a different story. Instead of berating myself further, I told myself this was rock bottom, and all I could do was grow and learn from this moment. *These* thoughts helped me pick myself up and start anew.

Our inner voice is an evolved capacity because it serves us well. It helps us simulate and plan, to coach ourselves along, and, importantly, it lets us tell stories so we can make sense of our lives. However, this inner voice can become toxic when we get stuck in a negative cycle. This is the dark side of the storytelling mind: We ruminate, we worry, we catastrophize, making this incredible self-talking capacity into a curse. We chew over that time we lost it with our child and end up flooded by shame. Then we think about it again and again, in a bleak cycle.

This kind of inner voice directly affects our parenting. Eventually this voice will come out to our children. I remember my mom looking in the mirror and telling herself how ugly she was. In my late teens I did the same exact thing.

Moreover, a harsh, judgmental inner voice strongly affects our ability to get back up and try again after making a mistake. When we judge our mistakes harshly, we are less likely to try again, more likely to remain stuck in an old pattern. But when we offer ourselves a softer landing after our inevitable human mistakes, it's easier to try again, so we grow and learn more quickly.

Perhaps the biggest problem with a harsh inner dialogue is how it pulls us away from the present moment. You could be in a flower-strewn field with your child, but if you're ruminating about your unpleasant conversation with a rude neighbor, those are the thoughts shaping your life experience. You're not really there.

Mindfulness meditation is a powerful antidote to all of this mind wandering. Your mindfulness practice *will* increase your capacity to drop rumination and bring your attention back into the present moment and to shift the *way* you're thinking.

We can't change what we're not aware of, so the first step is always mindfulness. What does the voice in your head say to you? Some of our thoughts are facts, like *It's sunny outside*; others are stories, like *I'm a terrible parent*. Mindfulness can make us aware of both kinds. Before we actually hear the inner discourse, the thoughts feel like reality. We can become fused with our thoughts so that they feel like they're *the truth*, incredibly *important*, and we must obey them.

Becoming mindfully aware of your thinking and recognizing thoughts for what they are—*words, images, and stories inside your head*—can help you *defuse*, or get a bit of space from your thoughts. Then you can decide whether they are helpful or unhelpful. You'll realize that you don't have to believe everything you think. Here's a simple, yet powerful tool that can help:

Unhook from Your Thoughts

Pick an upsetting thought that may have you hooked into believing it. Maybe you've thought *My child is trying to manipulate me.* Mentally put the phrase *I'm having a thought that...* in front of it. Silently repeat *I'm having a thought that...* coupled with your thought. You can also try it with the phrase, *I notice I'm having a thought that...* Notice whether this thought helps or hinders you. This will help you unhook from the thought and reduce its influence.

You can also use your inner voice to bring yourself back to more equilibrium.

Distanced Self-Talk

Use language to help yourself work through a difficult situation. Practice distanced self-talk by using your name and the second-person "you" to refer to yourself. For example, I might say to myself, *Hunter, you are thinking about work while you are walking with your daughter. Time to be here now.* This immediately interrupts the thoughts. You can imagine that you are advising a friend and give yourself that same advice.

Take action: When might these two tools become handy this week? What situations arise when unhelpful thoughts take over? Start to notice the tone of your inner dialogue and apply these two tools.

14

Can I Just Skip These Feelings?

From a purely biological perspective, we humans are feeling creatures who think, rather than thinking creatures who feel. —Jill Bolte Taylor

When I was yelling at my toddler, it felt *terrible*. My heart hurt. My shoulders were tight. I was short of breath. I was suffused with uncomfortable emotions, and I just wanted the feelings *to go away*. Yet I was experiencing that pain for a reason. It was showing me that things were out of balance and change needed to happen.

We experience pain for a purpose. It warns us of danger and signals us to take action. Negative emotions are *useful*. That small ping of anxiety before a big important event can help you prepare more. A zing in your gut may help you stay alert in a dark parking garage. Feelings are messengers, alerting us that something important needs our attention, keeping us safe.

What about anger? When anger arises in the context of parenting, it does not feel so useful. But it can be—when we channel the angry energy into action to make the world (or just our homes) a better place. On a Mindful Mama podcast episode, I talked about anger with Kristen Neff, researcher and author of *Fierce Self-Compassion*. I told her how many of us would like to erase any trace of anger from our system. She described anger as a "mama bear" energy that can be constructive. It focuses and energizes you, helps you draw boundaries, and suppresses the fear response. She explained that figuring out whether anger is destructive or constructive is very simple: *Does it help alleviate suffering, or does it make suffering worse?*

If you think of anger as a messenger, then you can learn from anger. Consider getting curious about what anger is telling you. Anger can be your teacher. But if you try to suppress or erase your anger, or if you shame yourself for having anger, you can't get curious about it or learn from it. You stay stuck and uncomfortable, hiding from what is actually happening, unable to solve any root problems.

Jill Bolte Taylor, neuroanatomist and author of *My Stroke of Insight*, tells us that we are primarily feeling animals that think (2006). So our feelings are clearly very important to our survival as a species. What is the brain doing with our emotions? Lisa Feldman Barrett, author of *How Emotions Are Made* and among the top 1 percent most-cited scientists in the world for her research in psychology and neuroscience, explains that the brain is up there in a dark box (our skull) interpreting the feelings and information sent to it from the senses (2017). If we have an uncomfortable, unpleasant feeling of chest tightness, our brain does not know whether it is indigestion, anxiety, or the beginning of a heart attack. The message: Something is out of balance and needs attention. The brain guesses at an explanation, using past experiences and information from the senses.

Imagine a graph with two axes: pleasant versus unpleasant and high arousal versus low arousal. If we have high arousal and high unpleasantness, we may feel anxious or fearful. If we have low arousal and low unpleasant feelings, we may feel depressed. High arousal and high pleasantness? Excitement!

Moreover, Dr. Barrett explains how the brain is running on what she calls a *budget*—it's taking the body's energy (glucose, salts, and so on) and allocating that energy to all the different body systems. An uncomfortable feeling often means we need more energy—something is out of balance. Think about how grouchy you are when you're hungry. This is your body running on empty—the grouchiness is a signal to get yourself back to a better balance.

Your feelings are a result of all of this information and interpretation. When you see them as message-bearers giving you vital information, it's easier to muster a bit more compassion for yourself. Chronic anxiety and stress are telling you something really important: You are extending yourself beyond your energetic budget, and you need more support.

In a culture that seems averse to emotional expression, we can look at our emotions pragmatically and see that they supply information, telling us whether we are in balance. You can see your children's feelings that way too—their behavior is communication about their present emotional state, giving you clues about their needs. If you can see emotions this way, it can dispel some of the drama. It's simply information: Don't shoot the messenger!

Take action: What are some unpleasant feelings that you regularly grapple with—in yourself or your child? If you view that feeling as information, can you get curious about the message that the feeling is sending?

15

Stuffing Is for Turkey

All the stuff that keeps you safe from feeling scary emotions? They also keep you from feeling the good emotions. You have to shake those off. You have to become vulnerable. —Brené Brown

As a child, when I was upset I was told to go to my room. Difficult feelings were something to suppress. Many of us had that experience. Now, as parents, we want to teach our children ways to handle their feelings, but few of us were taught how. We had just two ways to handle our difficult feelings: blocking or drowning.

Blocking is when you try to block or deny the discomfort by pushing through it through force of will. We do this by distracting ourselves (hello, smartphone!) or by self-medicating with food, alcohol, drugs, shopping, and the like. This is ultimately not helpful; as soon as you stop "pushing through" or your distraction or self-medication wears off, your uncomfortable feelings can come back even stronger.

When we stop blocking, we often swing to the other side of the pendulum and become overwhelmed by the emotion. We go into a downward spiral with thoughts like *I can't stand this!* or *How could they/I have been so stupid?* This leads to a sense of hopelessness and powerlessness. We're still not processing the feelings in a healthy way.

Mindful Mama podcast guest Curt Storring shared a wonderful metaphor for this. Imagine that you don't have a digestive system and you eat a big hamburger—an emotional hamburger. It's going into your body but isn't digested. Eventually someone is going to poke you and that hamburger will make a mess everywhere. Rather than blocking or drowning, we can learn to process our big feelings—our emotional hamburgers.

How do we digest our emotional hamburgers? We learn to *feel* the sensations of emotions but not get swept away by them. It takes practice, but the surprising and counterintuitive result of staying with an uncomfortable emotion is that the *I've got to get outta here* feeling often lessens, or even disappears. Instead of saying no to our difficult feelings, we start to say yes and practice to *accept* them.

You may not want to accept your feelings—saying yes may seem like a really bad idea. Why say yes? We practice acceptance because the feelings are here. Every single one of us will feel bad; that's part of life. When we consciously feel the feelings, we can process our emotions. Here are some ways to do it:

Name It to Tame It

Dr. Daniel Siegel coined the saying "Name it to tame it." When you notice you are having a strong emotional reaction, describe or name it—either to yourself or (even better) out loud to role model for your child.

For example, say "I am feeling frustrated" or "I can feel my heart rate rising and my shoulders getting tight." This helps you *see* the emotion rather than *be* the emotion. It can create some distance and relief.

You can also name it to tame it with your child. For example, if your child is frightened, you might say: "Wow, that was so scary! You didn't like that part of the movie." This helps your child feel seen, heard, and calmed. It also teaches helpful ways to process feelings.

Sometimes you need more than labeling your feelings. Psychologist, meditation teacher, and author Tara Brach teaches four powerful steps to process feelings:

R.A.I.N.

R.A.I.N. stands for "recognize," "allow" or "accept," "investigate," and "nurture." At first, you'll need a quiet space and some time to do this, but with practice, you can do R.A.I.N. to process feelings almost anywhere.

R – Recognize. Take a pause and mindfully breathe. Recognize that you are having a hard time. Recognize the sensations and feelings that are most prominent. You may notice a tight chest and shoulders. You might say to yourself, *upset, frustrated,* or *hurt.*

A – Allow/Accept. Give yourself a moment to be with this emotion and feel the sensations in your body. If you're noticing a lot of resistance—that *no!* feeling—you can try saying *yes, yes, yes* to yourself instead. It's okay that this feeling is here.

I – Investigate. Ask yourself *What really wants my attention right now? What am I thinking or believing right now?* Be curious about where this feeling came from, so that you can understand its message.

N – Nurture. Offer yourself kindness. You might put a hand to your heart. Say to yourself what you might say to a good friend: *It's okay, It's not your fault,* or even *I'm here for you.*

R.A.I.N. does not get rid of the feeling, but it helps you to process. When you take time to be with the difficult feeling, you will most often feel lighter, calmer, and wiser on the other side.

For those of us who were told not to have our difficult feelings, these tools can be a lifesaver. They have saved me from exploding at my kids, time and time again, because I was able to process my strong emotions rather than dump them on my kids.

Take action: Try a R.A.I.N. meditation this week to process any unresolved feelings that may be lingering. Then use "name it to tame it" in your daily interactions to up the emotional intelligence and lower the drama in your home.

16

A Better Way to Make Mistakes

Everyone knows we need to have mud for lotuses to grow. The mud doesn't smell so good, but the lotus flower smells very good. If you don't have mud, the lotus won't manifest. You can't grow lotus flowers on marble. Without mud, there can be no lotus. —Thích Nhất Hạnh

Even with all of the emotional processing tools on the planet, from time to time you are still going to mess up, make mistakes, and yell at your kids. I do—and not only do I teach Mindful Parenting, I teach others to teach Mindful Parenting! Mistakes are a part of the process of being human. As we have discussed, perfection in parenting is not an option. So if difficulties and mistakes are inevitable, what do we do with these mistakes? What do we do with our pain, our difficulties? We use them as *compost*.

One of the most valuable lessons I've heard from the world-renowned mindfulness teacher, Zen master, and peace activist Thích Nhất Hạnh is "no mud, no lotus." The lotus flower pushes through the muck, a lengthy and dark process that requires patience and understanding. Similarly, if you tend a garden, you know that the best food for healthy flowers and vegetables is *compost*—well-rotted vegetable matter and poop (from cows, chickens, rabbits). The gross, dark, slow-to-develop composting process is necessary for the brightest, healthiest flowers and the most flavorful, nutritious vegetables.

Just like the lotus or your cucumbers, humans, too, need darkness to recognize the light. Our challenges shape us, giving us more depth and compassion, which we can then give to our kids. The things we perceive as negative (conflicts, arguments, mistakes) can add value to things we believe are positive (close relationships, openness, and connection). Our difficulties, errors, and lapses can ultimately *help* us become kinder, more skillful, and more compassionate.

Think about it: If you never made your own mistakes, then you would have zero compassion for others' mistakes, because you wouldn't understand why on earth they would act that way. If we don't accept our own difficulties, darkness, and mistakes, we can become filled with judgment, and others will find us insufferable. High in our tower of perfection, we're critical of everyone and completely unable to connect with and understand our fellow humans.

In author and researcher Brené Brown's viral 2010 TED Talk, she talks about her research breakthrough identifying that *vulnerability*—the discomfort of uncertainty, risk, and emotional exposure—is in fact the *birthplace* of our most profound feelings, including joy, creativity, belonging, and love. She observes that we cannot selectively numb our emotions—when we numb grief, shame, and fear, we also numb joy and happiness. No mud, no lotus.

It's clear that living and parenting wholeheartedly requires us to accept our challenges, difficulties, and mistakes. Perhaps it's as the poet Kahlil Gibran wrote in his 1923 classic *The Prophet*: "The deeper that sorrow carves into your being, the more joy you can contain."

These words may strike a chord with you, yet deep down, many of us still have lots of trouble accepting our all-too-human faults and mistakes. But there is hope. The human mind has *neuroplasticity*—what you practice grows stronger. Try the following simple exercise to become more accepting of yourself. I started this practice many years ago, and it has helped me *every day* since then.

Loving Self-Acceptance

Loving self-acceptance can be practiced! It's okay if it feels uncomfortable and *really* corny. We can accept that too.

To cultivate self-acceptance, repeat this phrase to yourself, ideally while looking in the mirror, five times: "I love and accept myself exactly as I am."

If that phrase is too difficult for you, begin with "May I": "*May I* love and accept myself exactly as I am."

Try this practice for two weeks, then see how you feel. If it's helping, keep going! The positive effects will ripple out to your family, your community, and the world.

It's okay for you to have mud. Remember that you can transform those rotting plants and cow poop into a powerful compost that will nurture the flowers of joy, love, and connection in you.

Take action: Every day this week, repeat the Loving Self-Acceptance statement five times to yourself in the mirror. Remember, it takes time and patience for flowers to grow. We don't give up on them because they haven't bloomed yet!

17

My Parent's Voice Is Coming Out of My Mouth

Parenthood...it's about guiding the next generation and forgiving the last. —Peter Krause

As adults *without* children, we think we have it all figured out. Then we have kids. Suddenly, we're back in the parent-child relationship all over again. To our horror, we hear the things our own parents said *coming out of our mouths*. For me, it was my father's temper and his tendency to threaten. Yikes.

We are all the products of what our own parents modeled (which came from their parents, and so on). Unfortunately, we tend to repeat the unhelpful patterns of the past. There's a saying: "What we don't transform, we transmit."

Stuff from our childhood can directly impact how we parent our children, unpredictably interfering in that relationship. Take a parent who grew up in a highly dysfunctional home with lots of yelling, where the children's feelings were largely ignored. When that child becomes a parent herself, she unconsciously continues those dysfunctional patterns. She was ignored as a child, so when her own child ignores her, it triggers unresolved issues: feeling ignored, worthless, dismissed, and disrespected, leading to anger and yelling.

To stop the cycle, this parent needs to know that her own issues are at play here. She needs to know that her child is *not* telling her she is worthless; kids just don't like being told what to do. It's up to the parent to make the unconscious issues conscious and stop the cycle.

The key to letting go of our emotional baggage is mindful awareness. When our baggage is largely unconscious, we can't do anything about it. So we focus on our locus of control: ourself. To parent consciously, we must delve into our upbringing.

How to Deal with Our Triggers

1. **Uncover and understand them.** Reflect on your childhood, by yourself or with a therapist. What was communication and discipline like in your family? How did your own parents deal with upset feelings and anger? And how many of their attitudes have been passed on to you? In my first book, *Raising Good Humans,* I offer questions to explore.

2. **Notice when you're triggered.** Your mindfulness practice will help you see more clearly. Practice being aware of when your shoulders get tense, your child's behavior feels unbearable, and you are ranting inside your head. *Track* your triggers: Is there a pattern that you can discern? Particular times of day? When you're hungry?

3. **Get curious: What's really happening here?** Ask yourself *Am I overreacting to this situation?* If it's not

an emergency, then take a minute to remove yourself from the situation, process your feelings, and get curious.

Uncovering and healing our personal lingering issues helps us become freer, clearer, and able to be more present with our children. We also need to look at unhelpful ways of thinking from the larger culture.

In Western cultures, many parents believe—consciously or not—that children should be instantly obedient. When children resist commands, they are trying to "manipulate." Many well-meaning parents and educators believe that toddlers "throw a tantrum" intentionally. Collectively, we think that children have a lot more control over their emotions and behaviors than they actually do. We look at "bad" behavior as if they do it on purpose.

While some behaviors *are* on purpose (your four-year-old looks at you, picks up the glass of water, then slowly pours it onto the floor—what will happen?), many actions we deem "bad" are the result of a child's nervous system reacting to a perceived threat or their body being unable to process any more. Just like adults, kids can feel overwhelmed and stressed, and many of their undesirable actions stem from the fight-or-flight response. The ability to control emotions and behaviors isn't fully developed until early adulthood!

In *Body-Brain Parenting*, psychologist Mona Delahooke helps us look for the signs that behavior may stem from the fight-flight-freeze response:

- Fast, impulsive movements, constant motion, or running away
- Hitting, kicking, spitting, jumping, or throwing things
- Shallow, fast breathing
- High-pitched, loud, hostile voice or out-of-control laughter

Recognizing these as a stress response (rather than "on purpose" choices) helps us help kids regulate their out-of-control feelings. Compassion is more effective than yelling, ignoring, or punishing. We'll talk more about effective responses later, but for now let's understand that the idea that our child has control in these moments is wrong.

I had emotional triggers from my childhood. I believed that my daughter cried to "get to me." These were issues I'd never had to deal with before becoming a parent. I never thought about our cultural ideas about children, and I certainly didn't want to delve into my upbringing. Yet doing this work helped enormously. It may seem daunting, but when the fruit of your efforts is a stronger, more compassionate relationship with your child, isn't that worth it?

Take action: How were you parented? Start to ask yourself about the beliefs—from your family or culture—that may be driving your thinking.

18

How Can I Let It Go?

You are imperfect, you are wired for struggle, but you are worthy of love and belonging. —Brené Brown

Once, when my daughters were little, my parents came to visit. After the girls went to bed, I ended up in the guest room with my parents, chatting. In a moment of relaxed openness, my dad told me how he appreciated what I was doing with my girls. He talked about when he was a child, how his father beat him with a belt, and when I was little, he spanked me. Now I was not only not hitting my daughters, but raising them with compassion. His honest sharing helped me see and understand him better. The way he was treated as a child, although normal then, would be considered abuse today. His own suffering had led to his hurting me. Understanding led to forgiveness.

When we uncover our emotional baggage, many of us go through a period of anger at our parents. Their actions or words may have hurt us deeply. Ultimately, anger is part of the process, but it won't heal our pain.

My anger strained my relationship with my father for years, stemming from my hurt. When I was a little kid, I would cower behind the door as he raged down the hallway to spank me. As a

teenager I attempted to escape into drugs and partying, and our fights were epic. A decade after leaving their house, as I began my own mindfulness practice, I finally came to better understand us both. I could see how his suffering drove him to treat me that way—prompted by defense strategies he developed as a child when attacked by his own father. I was determined to stop this unhealthy cycle. Seeing his suffering clearly, how could I not forgive him?

Forgiveness is often wrongly understood. You do it not for other people, but for *yourself*. You're not letting anyone off the hook; you're freeing yourself. Ruminating on old hurts leaves us stuck in a cycle of negativity. It's like drinking poison and expecting the other person to suffer the toxic effects. As we heal, we free ourselves from endlessly experiencing this hurt. Forgiveness helps. Moreover, forgiveness is good for us: One study found that after forgiveness training, blood pressure was lower and people report needing fewer medicines, having better sleep, and physically feeling better (Swartz 2014).

Letting go of hard feelings toward another person is one of the most important skills we can learn to sustain healthy relationships. But how do we let go? We must put ourselves in their shoes. Practicing mindfulness helps. If someone has hurt us in some way, we can get curious as to *why*. What causes, conditions, defenses, and wounds drove that person to act badly?

Forgiveness helps us parent more skillfully. Because we're human, our immediate family members will sometimes act badly, and we will too. Forgiveness is a way to process that hurt and release it. I've found the forgiveness mantra to be extremely helpful:

Forgiveness Mantra/Prayer

This deeply healing, age-old practice from Hawai'i is called "Ho'oponopono" ("cause things to move back into balance"). You can use it like a mantra or a prayer, repeating the words and inviting the feeling inside.

> *For another:* I forgive you; I'm sorry; Thank you; I offer you love

> *For yourself:* I'm sorry; Please forgive me; Thank you; I offer you love

When done sincerely, it creates one of the most freeing sensations there is, like an invisible weight has been lifted.

It's okay if you're not ready for forgiveness. To invite that readiness, you can work with "May I be ready and open to forgive" for a few weeks or months.

Forgiveness is not weak or naive; it requires courage. We do not necessarily forgive and forget. We may forgive and hold strong boundaries around our time and energy with the person who hurt us. We can resolve to never again allow these harms to come to ourselves or another. Forgiveness does not even mean that we have to continue to be in a relationship with the one who hurt us. It may be the wisest choice to cut off contact.

Many of us suffer from our past, but ultimately we can see that it's painful to hold on to anger. Without forgiveness, we perpetuate the false idea that anger can heal our pain. With the practice of forgiveness, we let go and find relief.

Take action: Is there someone in your life whose actions or speech have hurt you, that you are open to forgiving? Start with the easiest thing to forgive, and try the Ho'oponopono mantra this week.

19

Parental Equilibrium in Three Easy Steps

Be patient with yourself. Self-growth is tender; it's holy ground. There's no greater investment.

—Stephen R. Covey

We thought that raising good humans would be all about the kiddos, but there is a lot of self-work to be done to shift away from old harmful patterns. Forgiveness, emotional baggage—oi! Add to that everyday life, which is already stressful. You may be dealing with any number of challenges, from financial, to family, to safety, and more. If we have a *chance* of being more present for our kids, we need every calming tool available. We need to be able to soothe ourselves to regain equilibrium after the nervous system goes haywire.

Most of us, especially those with children, are familiar with soothing others when they are upset or afraid. However, when we are triggered or stressed as adults, it can be difficult to regulate ourselves. We're often distracted and unaware how much tension and stress we're holding. As you practice mindfulness, you may start to become *more* aware of that tension. Ignorance is *not* bliss—but now you can remedy the problem with self-soothing.

Self-soothing helps reset your body's systems after a stress response and regain a healthy state of balance. When we hurt, we want to feel better. All people need soothing after an upset. We can see it in babies who soothe themselves by sucking on a thumb. Common adult self-soothing behaviors include reaching for an alcoholic drink or a tub of ice cream. However, these kinds of self-soothing behaviors can cause a cascade of additional problems. Instead, we can start to replace these unhealthy patterns with a self-soothing toolkit.

Comforting yourself may feel like unfamiliar territory. You may not know how to do it or even feel guilty about focusing on yourself. Many of us were raised to believe that putting others' needs ahead of our own is admirable. Yet, as we've seen, this idea is bad for kids, as we give our kids less than our wholehearted selves, and bad for parents, as we end up overwhelmed and burned out. I hereby give you permission and encouragement to take care of yourself—to soothe your nervous system—so that you can show up fully for your kids and your life.

Practice Self-Soothing

Read through these fifteen self-soothing practices and underline or check the ones that call to you. Then write five of them on each of three sticky notes and place them where you'll see them when needed.

1. Drink a cup of hot tea.
2. Listen to nature/bird sounds.
3. Read a novel.
4. Take a shower or bath.
5. Walk outside, preferably in a natural setting.
6. Stretch or practice gentle yoga.
7. Diffuse essential oils or light a candle.
8. Get a massage, or self-massage.
9. Listen to affirmations.
10. Distract by watching a comedy.
11. Do some deep breathing (like the 4-7-8 breath).
12. Write in your journal.
13. Enjoy self-sex or sex with a partner.
14. Listen to a soothing playlist.
15. Dance or do other exercise.

Currently, many kids see parents modeling how to drink too much alcohol or overeat to self-soothe. I remember watching my mom down a tub of gummy worms! Later, in high school and college, I mimicked the behavior that was modeled for me and binged cookie dough to feel better. Not such a healthy habit. If you have some unhealthy self-soothing habits, there's no need to shame and blame yourself. But you can start using this list to crowd out those unhealthy habits.

It is not selfish, egocentric, or weak to practice self-soothing; it's a wise and skillful choice that ultimately helps everyone in the family have a more peaceful existence. When our kids see us practicing healthy self-soothing, they often take up these kinds of behaviors. As ever, 80 percent of parenting is in modeling, so what do you want to model for your kids?

Take action: Write on sticky notes five of the self-soothing practices from this chapter to remind you that you have permission to soothe yourself. Try one of them today.

20

How to Stop Seeing Yesterday's Child

Begin to see what is in front of you, rather than what you learned is there. —Stephen C. Paul

When Maggie was almost three and I was five months pregnant with my second daughter, I went away for a week to an artist's retreat center in Vermont. It was fruitful artistically, but hard, because it was the longest I'd been away from my child in her short life. The day I came home, Maggie jumped into my arms and must have given me about two hundred kisses in our intense and wonderful reunion. I was overcome with surprise, because I could finally hear her voice as others heard it: adorably high-pitched. The distance gave me a perspective that I otherwise never would have had—I was able to see and hear her with fresh eyes (and ears!). It was a gift.

We don't have to go away for a week to be able to shift our perspective (although parenting breaks to refresh your energy are a good idea). In any moment we can bring curiosity and openness to our parenting. This is the Zen teaching of "beginner's mind"—a mind open to everything.

Beginner's mind is an orientation of being a true beginner so that we can learn and be fully open to the present moment. Think about it: We've never, ever been in this moment before—it's absolutely new. Even if you are rereading this passage, you are a different person in a new present moment in which everything has changed. If just twenty-four hours have passed, then your body has turned over fifty to seventy billion cells, 365,000 babies were born around the world, and 8.6 million lightning strikes have occurred. You are in a new moment you've never been in before, and so is your child.

Normally, we bring so many thoughts, habits, and desires to each moment that we often can't allow ourselves to see things afresh. We're so caught up in our preconceived ideas, labels, and judgments that in interactions with our children we cannot really see them. There's no room for novelty or new possibility. We're often stuck in our ideas about what we like or don't like or wanting to control a situation's outcome. When we choose the orientation of freshness instead, we can see our children as they are in this moment and be more open to possibilities.

Practicing beginner's mind can help you avoid *confirmation bias*—the mind's tendency to seek out information that supports views we already hold. Confirmation bias makes us easily accept new information that is consistent with our beliefs, but strongly question information that contradicts them. For instance, if you believe that your child is trying to "manipulate" you, you are likely to interpret their behaviors to support that idea. Confirmation bias can lead us to the wrong conclusions. Let's clean our lenses instead.

Beginner's mind does not mean we chuck all our life lessons or walk into dangerous situations. Rather, it's about bringing *curiosity* or even *awe* to this moment. What if we can see our children as if we've been away for weeks, so we start to see their magic and beauty?

What if we see our children and even ourselves without all of the stories and judgments, but with fresh eyes? How do we practice letting go of preconceived notions and being more open?

Practice: See Your Child with Fresh Eyes

Imagine you're just meeting your child for the first time. See them with fresh eyes, curious about who they are, as if you haven't known them all of their life.

Really look at your child: their hair, their smile, their clothes and shoes, the way they move their body. Be curious. Try to see details you might not normally notice.

Notice the way your child interacts with others with an attitude of curiosity rather than judgment. Pay close attention and allow yourself to be surprised.

I invite you to start fresh from here, today. This day, with this breath, you can begin anew—as best you can, let go of the past and see each new moment as exactly what it is: a new moment. Savoring and appreciating the world not only feels good but also reduces stress and helps us see problems—and our kids—more clearly (and less judgmentally).

Take action: Try this practice this week. It will help you get out of autopilot mode and into a place of presence and curiosity. And remember, what you practice grows stronger.

21

How to Pause

When we pause, we can notice the actual experience, the pain or pleasure, fear or excitement. In the stillness before our habits arise, we become free to act wisely.

—Jack Kornfield

When I was seriously struggling, I found out that step one from every parenting coach is to *pause*. Presented as an easy alternative option—just choose to do it!—this was very frustrating advice. I was ready and willing to pause—*I really wanted to pause*—but while in my stress response, it just wasn't happening.

How do we take that pause when our kid is freaking out, our own cortisol levels are spiking, and we are about to lose it? In these tough moments, it's a big ask to pause. But I found out that it can be done.

Pausing means releasing our forward movement so that we can create space to become aware. It's enormously helpful in parenting, because in times of challenge our actions are often propelled by generational habits, traumas, and issues that have little to do with the current problem. For instance, if you were always dismissed and never heard as a child, when your kid ignores you it can feel like a spring has popped, and unresolved bits of anger and frustration push you forward. This is parenting at its worst—unconsciously reacting from our stress response.

Pausing enables us to make a *choice* by bringing the PFC back into play to control our impulses. We see the options and gain time to sort through all the stories and needs at play. Pausing allows everyone's energy to settle a bit.

We may recognize its value, but how do we do it? Pausing is like any skill or habit: a muscle that we develop through *practice*. Meditation is like a formal, daily practice of pause—taking a break from the forward momentum of *doing* and practicing just *being*, with all the thoughts and sensations that go along with that. In meditation, we become familiar with resting with our body sensations—feeling our heartbeat, pulse, breath, any muscle tightness—so that when we're in a more challenging situation, we have practice with remaining nonreactive despite urgent body sensations. With a daily practice, we remind our body and mind at regular intervals that we can stop the unhealthy cycle of constant, rushed action.

We can also practice pause deliberately. Oren Jay Sofer, a meditation and nonviolent communication teacher, talked to me on the podcast about practicing pause in our communication with our kids. He suggested that we can consciously pause in the easy, nonproblematic times, to cultivate the habit and strengthen our pause muscle for the more difficult times.

In the vast majority of our interactions with our kids, we don't need to respond right away. The stress response makes us feel like we *have* to, but it's much better to walk away from our kids than lose it with them. We can make a goal of pausing, and as we become more practiced, we can even say what we're doing out loud: "I need a break right now." "I need to breathe for a minute." That's not *weak*; that's skillful role modeling.

Our practice of pause will help our children regulate their emotions too. Our emotional world is an open system, so we feel and are affected by each other's emotions. Small children especially depend on their parents' relative stability and groundedness to regulate their own feelings (picture a toddler running to Mama for comfort). When we cultivate the habit of pause, we can *be* that grounding, calming presence for our children. Without our *doing* anything, our open and accepting presence helps our children calm down. Our children borrow our calm.

If you're not naturally some kind of super-chill person, don't worry. I was far from that myself! Your regular mindfulness meditation practice and practicing the pause will cultivate your ability to be present. With a little bit of practice, soon you'll be able to demonstrate that power of pause in helping your child.

Practice Parental Pause

1. Stop moving. Ground your feet or sit down.
2. Place a hand on your heart.
3. Take a deep breath. Maybe another two deep breaths.
4. Slowly sit or kneel near your child.
5. Be present. Be still. Be curious.
6. Remind yourself: *My child is not* bad; *they are just struggling to cope with their world. This is developmentally normal. Let me be what they need right now—a safe, calm mountain.*

With practice, you will become more comfortable with simply being still and observing. You'll be less inclined to fill up all the spaces with action, talk, and doing. This gives your child a profound *permission* to be comfortable in their own skin and to rest.

Take action: This week, notice if you are filling all the spaces with talk or action. Take from a few days up to a week to practice pausing a beat before responding in calm times. If applicable, practice the parental pause in a challenging moment.

22

Grandpa Had This Wrong

Where did we ever get the crazy idea that in order to make children do better, first we have to make them feel worse? Think of the last time you felt humiliated or treated unfairly. Did you feel like cooperating or doing better?

—Jane Nelsen

When my second daughter was a month old, we met another family and talked about parenting. I was totally shocked to learn that they did not use punishments—not even time-outs—with their four kids. It sounded irresponsible to me—*I* was *not* going to have children who run roughshod over everyone, totally undisciplined! I didn't know then that time-outs just make children angrier and more dysregulated. Yet I did know that I wanted to parent differently from my father.

Although he has so many wonderful qualities, my father used traditional punishments to discipline me, and it ultimately created a deep chasm in our relationship. We had once been close through a shared love of art-making, but as an adolescent I felt only disconnection and anger. This rift lasted for over a decade, until I was able to forgive him, realizing that he was repeating the patterns from his past because he didn't know better. Ours is not an uncommon story; many people still have deeply damaged relationships with their parents because of the traditional strategies they used.

Punishment is still the norm, and many of us firmly believe that for our children to learn we have to reprimand and scold. Children are expected to be totally submissive to the higher authority of their parents. Why? Because parents will use their greater size and power to hurt them physically or mentally/emotionally. When I was little and made my dad angry, he spanked me. My fear of his anger kept me in line—or did it?

Yes, in the short run, your child likely will comply with an angry threat. However, it's not very effective in the long run. Using fear and threats actually makes your child *less* likely to cooperate and *more* resistant in the future, because punishment focuses your child on the pain they're feeling rather than on the effects of their behavior on someone else. It actually makes your child a little *more* selfish than before, because they're thinking, *Oh, I am feeling badly. I'm suffering. I'm mad at Mom and Dad*. Now the child is angry, concentrating on their own suffering, instead of the harm their actions caused. It makes them more self-centered.

Yelling and punishment do not teach "good" behavior; they teach your child to avoid more punishment in the future. Instead of motivating them to have more consideration for others, it teaches them to sneak around to escape detection. Punishment fosters dishonesty, teaching them to lie so they don't get caught.

Finally, punishments—yes, time-outs are punishments—erode your relationship with your child, making your child *less* likely to want to cooperate with you in the future. The less connected you are to your child, the worse their behavior becomes.

Research corroborates the negative effects of fear- and threat-based parenting. In a study that tracked nearly 1,500 students over nine years, researchers from University of Pittsburgh studied "harsh" parenting—tactics that include frequent yelling, hitting, and threats—and found that it may bring out the worst in teens' behavior (Sturge-Apple et al. 2012). Kids who were parented harshly in seventh grade were more likely to turn to their peers in unhealthy ways, such as hanging out with friends instead of doing homework, or engaging in early sexual behavior. More research shows that spanking—which, as of this writing, is still widely practiced around the world—is associated with increases in mental health problems in childhood and adulthood, delinquent behavior in childhood and criminal behavior in adulthood, negative parent-child relationships, and increased risk that children will be physically abused (Gershoff 2013).

Look again at the epigraph from Positive Discipline founder Jane Nelsen that begins this chapter. Although fear- and threat-based parenting has been the norm in Western cultures for centuries, when we look at it through the lens of relationships, it doesn't make a lot of sense. We know that kids are sponges and mimics, yet what are we modeling? That the most powerful, most aggressive person gets their way. That to "win," we can and should make others hurt and embarrassed. How can we expect kids to care for our needs and respect us if we don't model that for them?

What works instead? Modeling, guidance, and teaching. Doing better requires a mindset shift—a change of intention. I want my children not to just learn how to win at all costs, but to be able to cooperate with others—to respect themselves and others. We need to shift our mindset to see that we are always modeling, and our kids are always learning.

Take action: Were you raised with punishment? What was the effect? What is your intention for your kids? What do you want to model?

23

Don't Shout "Stop Yelling!"

You can learn many things from children. How much patience you have, for instance. —Franklin P. Jones

It's bedtime, and I am tired. It's been a long, exhausting day, but my kids aren't sleepy; they're hyped up! They're not listening to me, and I find myself shouting at them to calm down. Suddenly I go from rational parent to psychopath, yelling, "Stop shouting! Be quiet and go to bed already!" I must look like a crazed woman, because my daughters look at me with huge, scared eyes and start crying.

We all yell. In fact, a 2003 study found that 90 percent of parents admitted to angry shouting (Straus and Field 2003). It's universal in the US, yet yelling as discipline is not only *not* effective (we're not exactly teaching useful conflict resolution skills when we yell), but it often leads to the very outcomes we want to avoid. A 2013 long-term study found that harsh verbal discipline doesn't stop problem behaviors for tweens and teens and could make them *more* likely to continue doing whatever it is you are freaking out about (Wang and Kenny 2013).

From a kid's point of view, yelling is aggressive and scary. It seems like it "works," but we get results from yelling because they're scared and they just want us to stop yelling. It's *not* because they've actually made a choice to change their behavior. In the long term, yelling causes kids to shut down instead of listening, and to tune us out.

So how do we stop? I wish it were as easy as a simple choice. Yelling can be triggered by our stress response, so a hugely effective step is to reduce our overall reactivity with mindfulness (chapter 9). In the heat of the moment? Rather than a simple choice, reducing our yelling starts out first as an intention, then a behavior you practice (a lot). Then it becomes a habit, which finally turns into second nature. We are training the brain into a different response, and it's completely doable.

First, set an intention of calm for the moments when you've been stressed and shouty in the past. Consider bedtime. Often, we parents approach bedtime with demanding, yelling, and a generally raised energy, so *that's* what we're modeling for our kids. This is *not* what we want at bedtime. Instead, set the intention to be calm, sleepy, and in tune with your body's tiredness cues. Your intention can be powerful.

Second, it's important to know your triggers. This may be as simple as remembering that when you're hungry or tired, you yell easily; then you can be extra vigilant and ask for help at those times. As we discussed in chapter 16, we also get triggered by events in our past. Recognizing this is vital to being able to choose a different response in that moment. When I get triggered, I try to say to myself, *Hello old friend [frustration, not being listened to, whatever this trigger is], I see you there.* This simple, kind acknowledgment helps enormously! It's also backed by research that shows naming our emotions—the more specific, the better—reduces our distress and helps us calm down faster (Kashdan, Barrett, and McKnight 2015).

If you find yourself in a stressful moment, about to get shouty, it's completely fair to warn your kids. For example, if they are stalling at bedtime, you might say, "I'm starting to feel frustrated, and I don't want to yell to get your attention. If you don't listen now, I'm worried I'm going to lose it." You can also try crouching down to their level and dropping your voice to a whisper to get their attention in a totally different way.

Finally, when you find yourself about to yell or in a situation when you frequently yell, use all the resources in this book to calm down your stress response so you can choose a better way to respond. Take a break; use the 4-7-8 breathing from chapter 6. Write a list of calm-down responses on sticky notes and place them strategically. *Visualize* yourself using these instead of yelling, so your brain can practice ahead of the stressful moment. Remember, what you practice grows stronger—you can use your mind to shift your brain!

Here's another great resource to add to your sticky notes—mantras (short sayings you repeat to yourself) for those tricky parenting moments:

Calm-Down Mantras

What do you say to yourself when you feel overwhelmed by parenting? *This is too much*? *I can't handle this*? Instead, use these short mantras to calm down. Your kind words will let your nervous system know the "danger" has passed and allow the opposite relaxation response to kick in, allowing you to use your whole brain.

- This is not an emergency.
- I am helping my child.
- When they yell, I get calm.
- I am not alone in this.
- I am safe, and I can choose calm.

Take action: Add two mantras of your choice (along with other calm-down tools in earlier chapters) to four sticky notes that you place strategically around your home. Visualize yourself using these!

24

Logic Doesn't Work, But This Does

When a child is upset, logic often won't work until we have responded to the right brain's emotional needs.
—Daniel J. Siegel and Tina Payne Bryson

When my oldest daughter was eight, we embarked on what we thought would be a typical long drive to my parents' house to visit. The ride was stressful, but not as intense as the news phoned in from my parents: There was a health emergency with my grandparents, and my parents had to leave. We arrived at a strangely empty house, feeling anxious. Finally, it became too much for my daughter, who started yelling, then hysterically crying. I got her into a shower. Through the bathroom door I could hear her still crying. When her shower ended, I came into the steamy bathroom to hold her, wrapped in a towel. I "heard" her emotions by telling her the "story" of that day and how hard it was. I attuned to her emotions, held her, and helped process her feelings with compassion. As I told the story of the day, her crying subsided and she recovered.

As we talked about in chapter 7, kids coregulate their emotions with us. Consider that we humans don't fully develop the ability to control our emotions and behaviors until our early twenties! Yet we often overestimate children's abilities to self-regulate their feelings.

We often end up dismissing feelings that don't make sense to us (what's all the fuss about the wrong color cup?). We ask them to "use your words" when their actions clearly tell us that they don't have that kind of control. In short, we want to use talking, advice, and logic when what our children really need is for us to tune in to their feelings.

We parents experience a lot of frustration relating to our kids because we're not really listening to them. If we sense something is wrong with our child, we feel uncomfortable, anxious—we just want to solve their problem and make it go away. So we plow forward with our agenda, dismissing the feelings, or we seek to address the problem by controlling the conversation. It comes from a loving place, but ultimately always seeking to "fix" the problem of our kid's feelings sends the message that it's not okay to have uncomfortable or unpleasant feelings. We're communicating *non*acceptance.

Your child's deepest desire is for you to really see, hear, and accept them—for you to love them *unconditionally*. This acceptance gives them a feeling of safety and security, arming them to handle the challenges life throws at them, to learn, grow, and (gradually) emotionally mature. To be able to calm their stress response, kids need to feel safe and loved, and that has to happen *before* they can make any kind of behavior change. Feelings come first.

How, then, do we help our kids, if not through talking or fixing the problem? The solution is usually way simpler. Often, we don't have to *do* anything at all. We can simply be present and listen. We can slow our forward momentum, breathe, and tune in to ourself and our child. We offer them the energy of curiosity, rather than judgment, and compassionate acceptance rather than "I have to fix you." This kind of presence is the healing that our children seek. This is where your mindfulness meditation practice really comes in handy, because when you regularly practice present moment awareness, you can tap into that ability more easily.

Deep listening offers our children the kind of loving, accepting attention that provides the basis for security and resilience. When we listen with our full attention, kindness, and curiosity, reflecting back our understanding of their feelings—"Looks like you're feeling really upset now"—it helps kids become aware of what they are actually feeling. Naming the emotions helps to calm them down, but the real magic is that they feel truly seen and heard. Your loving presence, acknowledgment of their challenge, and full acceptance works far faster than jumping in to "fix" the problem. Try it and see.

Practice: Deep Listening

1. **Stop what you're doing.** Close the laptop, put down the phone, and orient your body toward your child (or whoever you are listening to). Take a conscious breath. Let go of your agenda as best you can. Bring yourself back to the present moment.

2. **Focus your attention on the speaker.** They are the object of your mindfulness. Bring an attitude of kindness and curiosity. Listen.

3. **If judgments, thoughts, arguments, and the like arise** (as they likely will), just notice them, don't judge them, then return your attention to the speaker.

4. **Be aware of your own felt senses,** like a knot in your belly or tight shoulders. Notice your own feelings and thoughts that arise.

5. **Don't rush to speak.** It's okay to have silence and a healthy pause before you speak. This is the space you need to respond compassionately rather than react on autopilot. Sometimes your response can simply be an empathetic sound.

Note: You cannot fake your calm presence. If you want to scream inside, it's better to walk away and calm your emotions instead of pretending (our kids have amazing b.s. meters).

Take action: Practice deep listening with your child this week!

25

I Don't Need to Entertain My Kid

In the tapestry of childhood, what stands out is not the splashy, blow-out trip to Disneyland but the common threads that run throughout and repeat: the family dinners, nature walks, reading together at bedtime...

—Lisa M. Ross

We come across this problem all the time as parents: We're trying to get something done, like making dinner, when our small child comes and wants attention, getting in the way. The little ones want to help, but we get the job done faster by ourselves. This is where we parents in Western cultures make a big mistake (I have, plenty of times): We shoo our small child away, telling them to go play with toys, or we give them some screen time entertainment. This sends them the message, again and again, that they should *not* be involved in taking care of the home. We teach them that they have special VIP status and their role is to be entertained.

The idea that kids need to be entertained is normalized and reinforced constantly by our culture. We want what's best for our kids, so when we live in a culture that says more is better, we buy into that—literally, with mountains of toys, books, and games that promise to make our children smarter and more creative. But in our abundant modern world, what if what's best for them is actually less?

What happens if we take that fabulous young child energy of "I want to help!" and say yes?

I'm going to suggest a radical notion here: Your everyday life of making breakfast, setting the table, cleaning the dishes, walking the dog, doing the laundry—even doing your work—may be all the stimulation your child needs. I have another radical notion for you: It's *good* for your child to be bored.

Many of us shrink in horror at the thought of our child whining, "I'm bored!" We see their boredom as a problem to be solved. It's not. If we respond to our kids' boredom by providing technological entertainment or structured activities, it teaches kids that they are *not* part of the team. We rob them of opportunities to tap into their imaginations. Think of boredom as a precursor to creativity. Our children *need* unstructured time to be able to hear their own inner voices and to explore their own passions, which is how they grow and develop their unique interests. If we keep them busy with lessons and structured activity, or if we "fill" their time with screen entertainment, they never learn to initiate the kind of deep, creative play that helps them know themselves.

When we give our kids screen time so we can get stuff done around the house, we not only teach them *not* to help, but we reduce their ability to do this kind of deep, creative play in the real, non-screen world. I encourage you to limit screen time so that your child can instead build their inner resources—their energy, creativity, interests, resiliency—as well as become a more helpful member of the home.

Give your child some unstructured, nonscreen time and you will see them rise to the occasion (after some minor complaining) and find something interesting to do with it. Without the overwhelming stimulation of screen time or too many toys, our children can be "entertained" by daily life. Rather than structuring your time around child-centered activities, try to bring children into your adult life. Children can watch while you do chores around the house and get involved in small ways. Folding laundry? Let your child play under the towels. Do they need to be put away afterward? Show your child how you fold and bring the towels to the shelves. Want to go for a picnic or a hike? Bring your child and adjust the level of activity so they can be involved. Yes, this takes more time, but instead of moving at our fast adult pace, we can slow down and make the everyday activity the main event.

Instead of feeling responsible to entertain your child, consider the time when they are young as a chance to slow down and do *less*—to instead focus on your daily life at the slower pace of childhood. You don't have to be the entertainer; just live your daily life and bring your child along for the ride.

Take action: Take half a day to schedule nothing and simply include your child in everyday tasks. Notice how you feel: It may be hard to slow down, and that's okay. Practice letting go of perfection and focusing instead on loving connection with your child.

26

How Do I Make Them Stop?

If the ability to control emotions and behaviors isn't fully developed until early adulthood, why are we requiring preschoolers to do this and then punishing them when they can't? —Mona Delahooke

My five-year-old daughter was screaming around the house, "flying" a big piece of cardboard. It knocked things off the coffee table, and the noise had me gritting my teeth. This had to stop, or I was going to lose it. But I'd just recently pledged not to use threats and punishments with her, so how the heck could I stop this? How do we hold boundaries without yelling and threatening?

When we move away from fear- and threat-based parenting, we sometimes swing to the other end of the spectrum, becoming uncertain and backing off altogether from holding boundaries with our kids. This does *not* work out well. Now, instead of our kids resenting us, it's likely *we resent them*! Plus, kids need healthy boundaries to feel safe and cared for. Permissive parenting—allowing kids to get their way most of the time—can lead to unwanted outcomes for kids. Research has shown that children who grow up with parents who don't uphold appropriate behavioral expectations are more likely to be more self-centered, lack self-regulation and impulse control, and have higher rates of drug use than other children (Shapiro and White 2014).

Boundaries are healthy and necessary *even if* you want to move from an authoritarian paradigm to a more democratic way of doing things. Think of yourself as the wise, benevolent leader setting rules and routines for mealtimes, bedtime, homework time, chores, screen time, and more. Let kids be kids—expecting them to be immature and unskillful—and give them limits to keep them healthy and safe and to honor our own human needs. For both the parents' sake and the child's, it's important to decide what those limits are ahead of time. Then when there's opportunity for freedom, we can allow it.

In our home, we had three overarching rules: (1) take care of ourselves, (2) take care of each other, and (3) take care of our home. Smaller rules and norms stem from these and help provide a sense of teamwork among the family—we do things this way, not that way. We put away our toys when we're done playing. We turn off the lights when we leave a room.

Running around and knocking things down with a big piece of cardboard was *not* taking care of our home (or helping me and my sanity). So how to deal with this? I had a big shift to realizing that I can hold these boundaries without being scary, harsh, and disrespectful. I could be *firm and kind*. Instead of yelling, I can catch my daughter and say "Whoa! Hold on a sec, honey. That cardboard is knocking things over," while I gently take it from her hand. I offer her an opportunity to run outside with the cardboard. She learns a better way to be in the world, and our relationship is not damaged. If I did not hold that boundary, I might have resented her behavior.

Mindful Parenting member Caroline wrote to me about how her little ones pull on her legs and fight over who gets to sit on her lap. She said to me, "Some days I am just touched out!" We talked about the need to hold a boundary here. While loving touch can be wonderful and connecting, we do not have to be touched when we don't want it. In fact, it's healthy role modeling to hold boundaries around our own bodily autonomy. Caroline can say something like "Right now I feel touched-out, and I need some personal space. Can I have a hug in a few minutes?" She can hold this boundary firmly, without being punitive, even if her kids push back, offering a gentle "No thanks," and repeating her message. When she does this, she models for her kids how to have safe and healthy boundaries for their own bodies.

Whatever the rules are in your home, be *consistent*—don't flip-flop on what the boundaries are. If you're telling them no screen time right before bed one night, only to cave in the next evening, you are sending a message that the rules don't mean much, don't need to be respected, and can easily be changed. Parenting is not about always keeping your child happy and comfortable. It's okay if they're upset. You can still hold your boundary, kindly and firmly.

As you set up some healthy boundaries and rules in your home, be *patient*. Don't expect kids to get it right away. It's normal for kids to need many (many!) reminders about a boundary before they get it. Expect kids to mess up and make mistakes. Our job is to gently guide them into the future—not to whip them into shape.

Take action: This week, take some time to ask yourself: What rules should we have? What's really important to our family?

27

Be Playful

Children don't say, "I had a hard day at school today; can I talk to you about it?" They say, "Will you play with me?" —Lawrence J. Cohen

When my oldest was two years old, she wanted me to play with her. Every. Single. Day. I disliked playing pretend, but I hated a certain board game involving candy even more. None of it was my cup of tea, yet her appetite for play was insatiable. She would lead, dictating the story line and the characters, and I would follow. Clearly, it was her way of exploring the world in an empowered way, so I managed my feelings about pretending and joined her world a little each day.

I'm glad I did, because free, unstructured play supports kids' creativity; builds social, problem-solving, and decision-making skills; and helps them cope with stress. Children use play to learn, to build confidence, and to heal from emotional distress. In fact, children are like many other mammals in that they spend huge amounts of time and energy playing with objects and engaging in pretend. Scientists believe that play may be critical for healthy development and survival.

We parents can forget that children speak the language of play. If we keep this in mind, we can use the power of play and playfulness to connect and even to hold boundaries, while avoiding soul-dampening power struggles. Our connection with our child is what drives them to listen to us, to consider our feelings, and ultimately to cooperate. Safety and connection lead kids to feelings of security and confidence. Moments of eye contact, touch, presence, and playful situations build bonds that help kids listen. Play and playfulness will make a huge difference in your parenting and relationship! I know, you're tired, but try it and see.

One way to connect that parents often skip over is active, physical play. Play like wrestling and roughhousing encourages impulse control, confidence, self-soothing, and paying attention. It benefits both boys and girls, kids who are active and those who are quiet. Try asking your child to try to get past you. It helps to transform powerlessness into confidence, and it can be so fun. Here are a few rules to follow from Lawrence Cohen's wonderful book *Playful Parenting*: make sure you keep it safe (no hitting, biting, punching, or kicking), take cuddle breaks, (usually) let your kid win, and stop immediately if someone's hurt or wants to stop. Look for giggles and exertion.

Play and playfulness help in an enormous variety of circumstances, ages, and stages. You can build confidence in your young child by letting them win at checkers. You can connect with your tween through a pillow fight. If there are two adults around, show your child your love with a mock child tug-of-war: "I want Olivia! You can't have her," while grabbing her arm. "I'll take her head!" "I get her feet!" You can imagine how this could lead to massive giggles and your child feeling very loved.

Being playful can help us reduce power struggles. Here are some ways to hold limits playfully:

- **Be a robot.** Or a Southern belle, or an English lord. Use a silly character voice to get your child to do everyday chores like toothbrushing or clearing the table. Practice your best robot voice and say, "The teeth. Need. To. Be. Brushed. Commencing toothpaste sequence."
- **Be incompetent.** Kids find it hilarious when you act as though you can't do basic things. "Oh no, I forgot how to leave this playground and I can't find the exit! Is it here? [bumping into a tree]?" "Time to brush our teeth! Wait, where are our teeth? Are they here [bringing toothbrush to ears or elbows]?" "Bedtime! I'm so tired! Let me lie down on this comfy bed [lying down on your child without hurting them]." This gets kids giggling and puts them in the responsible adult seat when they help you.
- **Be contrary.** In a silly, exaggerated way, demand that your child do the *opposite* of what you want them to do. "Please don't get in the tub. Don't do it! You know I hate it when you're clean! Ew, you're using soap!" Sometimes children resist our limits just because they feel powerless. Exaggerating the opposite stance allows your child to have some power.
- **Use goofy threats.** Instead of scary threats, head off a problem by being silly. Lawrence Cohen suggests this great

> "threat" in *Playful Parenting*: "If you do that again, I'm going to have to sing 'The Star-Spangled Banner.'"

Being playful can actually be a stress-reliever for the grown-ups, too. In fact, setting aside just ten minutes for some exuberant play at the end of the work day can help you unwind, meet your kids' needs for play, and let everyone reconnect. Blast a favorite song and sing while you make dinner. Dance around ridiculously while doing chores with your child. Kids desperately want us to loosen up and have fun, and when we do, everyone benefits.

Take action: In your next interaction with your child, try being silly and making them smile. Notice how it shifts the tone in a positive way.

28

Expect a Lot of Mistakes

There are no perfect parents, and there are no perfect children, but there are plenty of perfect moments along the way. —Dave Willis

When my oldest daughter was three, she was able to put on her own shirt. By the time she was almost four, she could put on every item of clothes by herself. Huzzah! I thought. From now on, she will get herself dressed, all by herself, all the time. Wrong. Just because she had the physical capability to do it didn't mean that she was ready to own that responsibility. My expectations were too high.

Having high expectations for our kids is generally considered positive to support them in reaching their potential. However, we hear stories of kids becoming potty-trained at six months or reading chapter books by age four. We want our kid to be exceptional too! We can get caught up in this competitive, achievement-oriented culture and inadvertently push kids too hard or demand that they behave in ways beyond their capability. Perhaps we were subjected to similar high expectations as children, and it's simply an unexamined habit to pass that on to our kids.

Our expectations are often way too high regarding kids' emotional maturity. My older daughter was verbally precocious, speaking in full, complete sentences at two, so I kept expecting her to be as mature as her sentences. I had unreasonably high expectations for her to be able to regulate her feelings when it just wasn't possible for her yet. This led to months of frustration on my part.

We forget that kids are *by definition* immature. They are going to make a lot of mistakes and need a lot of repetition to learn everything. Sometimes, when we get into an old-school way of thinking ("My child should obey my word instantaneously"), our expectation for their compliance with a request becomes higher than it would be for another adult. We forget that the PFC—the area involved in emotional regulation, impulse control, and logical thinking—is *not fully developed until a person's in their early twenties.* It's wildly unreasonable for us to expect preschoolers to manage their emotions and make logical choices, yet still we do.

Parents, we need to lower our expectations and expect a lot of mistakes. Learning anything new—from emotional regulation to reading, household chores to bike-riding—takes patient repetition, as well as trust that it will come in time. Even after a thing is learned, it's unreasonable to expect perfection. Give your child permission to be human.

One way to temper expectations is to learn about child development. I highly recommend Chip Wood's *Yardsticks*, which helps us understand development from ages four to fourteen. Here are some points to consider:

Infants and toddlers to age three: They need our loving interactions to soothe them again and again. A two-year-old shows independence from their parents but is not emotionally independent—they need to coregulate, or "borrow your calm." Name and acknowledge the emotions you and your child are feeling. Model healthy emotional regulation as best you can.

Preschoolers, ages three to five: They can make choices based on their own interests now. This is a great age to harness the "do it myself" energy to involve kids with household tasks. Give your child the language of emotions and normalize feelings. Kids continue to coregulate, but you can start to introduce strategies like the Calm-Down Kit (chapter 6).

School-age children, ages six to twelve: Kids have more emotional regulation and may play through emotions symbolically. They may get upset over injustice, criticism, or feeling rejected. They stop being self-centered and relate more with others' feelings. Continue to validate their feelings and actively teach emotional regulation strategies. Model healthy emotional regulation.

Adolescents, ages thirteen to eighteen: Body, mind, and emotions are changing quickly. One day they're as responsible and cooperative as an adult; the next they might seem more like a stubborn six-year-old. Adolescents need more independence and to know that the adults will keep safe boundaries. They still do not have fully developed emotional regulation or impulse control!

While kids' feelings deserve the same respect as adults, kids are not little grown-ups. Human brains take many years to become fully mature, and kids need our grounding, calming influence at every age. We can replace old-school habits of shaming our children with realistic understanding of their development.

Take action: Talk with your parenting partner or a friend about your expectations for your child. In what ways are they unrealistic? Is it okay to make mistakes?

29

How to Talk to Little Kids

I had to learn to listen more than I talked. I had to stop jumping in with my solutions or lessons. It was amazing how many tantrums in the grade-school years ended when I simply reflected what the kids were saying and showed that I understood where they were coming from.

—Katherine Reynolds Lewis

If you're like me, when your child was an infant you talked to them (at least sometimes) in a high-pitched, sing-songy voice. I sang songs to my daughter for everything—even for changing her diaper! We don't talk to other adults that way (how awkward would that be?), nor, I hope, teenagers. Yet we still have a cultural tendency to talk down to little kids or perform the *role* of Mom or Dad, rather than be authentic.

How do we talk to little kids? We want to model the kind of communication we expect: We should speak the way we want to be spoken to. Toddlers learn to talk through everyday interactions with others.

Children undergo a massive amount of brain development before age five. They are like sponges, taking everything in, and you are modeling how to interact with others. So it's important to be respectful in our interactions from the very beginning. Our communication goal should be that our kids feel secure, that someone is deeply, truly interested in them. We can treat even the youngest children as unique, interesting human beings and not objects or blank slates to be written on.

Here are some ways to communicate skillfully with little kids:

Be yourself. Treating children respectfully starts with respecting yourself. You are also a unique human being, more than simply a parent, so I encourage you to be yourself, not just the role of Mom or Dad. Don't refer to yourself in the third person, as in "Mommy is coming to put you to bed," or "Come take Daddy's hand." Use first person: "I," "me," "my," and so on. As they grow, kids learn that you are an individual with your own wants and needs—that's a good thing!

Speak simply and honestly. Children tend to tune out parents who talk too much. Use short sentences and simple words, keeping your child's developmental age in mind. You don't need to give long-winded explanations. If your child asks you a difficult question like "Why is the sky blue?," you can honestly answer, "I don't know! Let's go home and look it up later."

Connect, then correct. Before you have to give your child any instructions, crouch down to their level and wait until you have their attention. You can help them learn how to focus: "Willow, I need your eyes." "Asher, I need your ears." If you need to correct your child's behavior, make sure you connect first. This can be acknowledging the feelings: "You are really upset! You didn't like it when she took your ball." It can also be reminding the child how valuable they are to you, while holding a boundary: "I love you, and the answer is no." Be a patient coach on how to be a good human.

Be positive. Little kids live in a world of *can't*, *don't*, and *no*. Instead of focusing on what your child *can't* do, practice telling them what they *can* do. Positive language encourages and builds confidence. Instead of "Stop running!," say "Walk, please." Instead of "Don't hit your brother!," say "Use gentle touches." Instead of "Don't get out of your bed," say "I know you can stay in your bed all night." In general, you can use this formula: Instead of "Don't __________," say "I like it when __________."

Say please, thank you, and sorry. Remember, we are modeling all the time. Rather than having to teach your child to say polite words, just use them regularly. Thank your child when they do something helpful. Use "please" in your requests. Model apologizing too. Even little kids know that apologies aren't meaningful unless the transgressor actually means it. Instead of "Say you're sorry" you can simply apologize to your child when you've said or done something wrong. If your child has done something to another child on the playground, don't force the apology. Let your child calm down and talk through the situation later. It may mean that *you* have to go over and apologize instead.

Listen attentively. Listen *more* than you talk. When you put down the phone and give your four-year-old all of your attention to listen respectfully to their story, they learn that you are someone they can come to. They learn that you will really see and hear them. Practice this when they are little, and later your teen will talk to you.

Take action: Take one of these six suggestions and write it on four sticky notes to place around your home strategically this week, and practice!

30

Stop Barking Orders

When we give children commands, we're working against ourselves. Where we had hoped to inspire obedience, we've just stirred up rebellion in their little hearts.

—Joanna Faber and Julie King

My firstborn daughter, at two years old, put up major resistance to the way I was parenting her. She let me know through excruciating daily (sometimes hourly) tantrums, pushback, and defiance. It felt like I couldn't say anything to her! Later in her life, I was able to get some perspective from her point of view, and I'll share a bit of that.

Imagine you're a toddler, trying to get along in an obstacle course of a world where everything is made for beings that are three times as tall as you. Mentally and emotionally, it takes everything you've got to get through the day (thank goodness for all of those restorative hugs and snuggles). You are learning about yourself and your world, and your parents are constantly directing it: "Come here. Get down! Don't touch that! Put on your shoes. Take off your shoes. Get in the car. Get out of the car. Sit down. No, no! Get up. Give me your hand. Eat this. Give me that..." and on it goes.

Little kids get ordered around All. Day. Long. Don't believe me? Go to a playground and listen to the way parents talk to their toddlers, or better yet, put your phone on record for twenty minutes on a typical day at home. I guarantee you will hear a steady stream of orders and commands. The problem with this? We give directions way too often, and kids, just like people of every age, don't like being told what to do. Do you like being told what to do? I don't! Even if I want to do something, if my husband then tells me to do it, I don't want to anymore. It's human nature to oppose direct orders. Too many commands cause resistance, defensiveness, and contrary behavior.

So what do we do? First, *become aware* of how often you are giving direct commands. Take some time to listen to yourself. Do a twenty-minute recording on a typical day. Becoming aware that there's really a problem is the first step to changing it. This is a win.

Then you can practice being more skillful in engaging your kid to cooperate. There are many ways to do this! One of the simplest is to put your words through a filter: *Pretend your child is your friend's kid.* How would you engage them to cooperate with you? This filter helps because we're just naturally more considerate toward those we're not as close to.

Here are some other tools for engaging cooperation from Joanna Faber and Julie King's wonderful book, *How to Talk So Little Kids Will Listen*:

1. **Be playful.** Do you have to put shoes on? Make the shoes tell your child how much they miss their feet. The hungry toybox demands blocks to eat in a monster voice. Do your robot voice, a duck, or your best Southern belle. You can make it into a challenge: Hop on one foot back to the car to go. If you can muster a

little playfulness, you can make anything more inviting.

2. **Offer a choice.** Instead of being demanding, invite kids to have autonomy over things they can control. Instead of "Get in the car now!," offer your child the choice between bringing a stuffed animal or a book. Do they want to hold your hand or get a piggyback to the store?

3. **Give information.** Share the effects of their unskillful actions to give them the chance to work it out for themselves. For instance, instead of "Stop hitting the dog!," try "Hitting hurts her. She likes gentle touches." Instead of "Wear your bike helmet!," say "Bike helmets protect our heads, and it's the law too."

4. **Say it with a word.** When my daughter starts walking away from the dinner table, I can say, "Your plate," and she remembers to clear. Simply say "seatbelt" instead of giving an order. This can even be a gesture (finger to the lips to be quiet), but don't use a verb like "Sit!" or "Come!" Those are better for dogs than for kids.

5. **Describe what you see.** Nonjudgmentally describe the situation rather than issuing a command. "The backpack is on the floor blocking the door." "I see noodles on the floor." "I see toothpaste on the sink."

Then step back and give your child some time to rectify the situation.

As you start inviting your child to be helpful and cooperative, remember last chapter's message: Expect a lot of mistakes. Expect unskillful, immature behavior. Just because your child *can* do something doesn't mean that they will always be mentally and emotionally ready to cooperate. There will be many, many times that their developmental needs take precedence (in their mind anyway) over what needs to happen. Patient, nonjudgmental repetition is the key.

Take action: Pick one of the tools for engaging cooperation and practice it this week. Next week choose a different tool. Soon they'll all be in your toolbox!

31

How to Talk to Older Kids

When your child is little, all you want is for them to play alone in their room for an hour so you can have some peace and quiet. Then they become teenagers, and all you want is for them to come out of their room for an hour and actually talk to you. —Janene Dutt

When my older daughter was thirteen, occasionally she started giving me "the attitude"—she would talk to me in a dismissive way, her voice dripping with sarcasm. Cue my lion's roar of rage at being so disrespected. So here was the terrible teen behavior that every other adult I met warned against when I said I had two girls. I didn't want this dynamic to continue.

I quickly found out that reacting mindlessly and defensively did *not* work; it only escalated issues to a new, more combative level. What to do? I had to remember what I teach in Mindful Parenting: Calm my reactivity and be *honest*. I had to look inside, and I found that underneath my anger were hurt feelings and sadness. The next time she gave me the attitude, instead of raging, even though this was *really, really hard,* I opened up to my feelings of sadness and hurt. I honestly shared with her, "When you talk to me like that, I feel so sad and hurt. It feels like I can't talk to you." She didn't fight back. She didn't say anything. Yet this time the argument did not escalate, and within an hour we were able to reconnect.

Older kids and adolescents growing up today are dealing with a lot. Not only do they have the turmoil of normal development, but they deal with new societal and environmental uncertainties that only increase their experience of pressure and stress. They're establishing identity and autonomy, and while friendships become very important, and they do need their space, they also need their parents' grounding influence and support.

How do we talk to our older kids when they are actively pulling away? To stay connected to our kids, we need to walk the middle path between becoming overbearing and giving in. Our loving presence is just as important now as when they were little. It may be even *more* important to have open lines of communication—bigger kids have bigger problems. Research has shown that parent-teen communication is a key protective factor for teens, shaping everything from physical and mental health outcomes to school performance and self-esteem (National Research Council 2009; US Department of Health and Human Services 2009). We can practice not taking their developmentally normal turmoil personally and be the solid, safe support that they return to.

Here are some suggestions for healthy communication with your older child:

Be authentic. Older kids and adolescents have amazing B.S. meters. Don't pretend to be calm when you're angry. I find it better to say, "I can't talk now" than to try to be calm when you're not. Be real and share your authentic feelings, as long as it's safe to do so (you may be authentically losing it, but that's when you want to practice restraint).

Also, be yourself. Don't try to talk to them the way their friends would.

Let them know you care. You can be tempted to respond to an "I don't care" stance from your child with the same attitude. That closes off the lines of communication completely. Instead, be the adult in the relationship and show your child that you care. Like with my daughter's attitude, you'll find that being real and vulnerable opens up the lines of communication.

Listen attentively. When your child is little, they tell you about everything *all* the time. Not so with older kids and teens. So when they want to talk, if you can, drop everything and listen. Put the phone down, close the laptop screen, orient your eyes and body toward them, and as best you can, be present (as we discussed in chapter 24). Practice letting go of judgments and criticism; be open-minded. By listening, you show your child that you love them, you are there for them, and you accept their thoughts and feelings.

Make time together. Your child isn't little anymore, clamoring for your attention, so it's important to build regular time together into your routine. I highly recommend holding onto a regular family meal time with no screens around. This can be challenging with sports practices and schedules—not to mention different dietary requirements! Overcome those obstacles to sit down together as regularly as you can. During meals you can share a "rose, thorn, and bud" from the day (something positive, something negative, and something you're looking forward to) to get the conversation rolling.

You can take your older child on a "date," to bring you closer together, just as you would with your partner (see chapter 37). Take them out for ice cream; invite them on a hike. Don't give up on spending time with your teen or inviting them into relationship with you. It's not a time to just "get through;" it's a time to cherish.

Take action: Write down five ideas for taking your older child on a date and suggest one to your child today!

32

Be a Calm Mountain

Whatever the situation, we cannot make peace unless we ourselves are peaceful. —Thích Nhất Hạnh

My two daughters had been playing happily, but when it was time for bed, the younger daughter started to get revved up. Suddenly she was flying around her room, yelling. I was exhausted, but my previous nights' tactics of demanding that she settle down had *not* worked. They'd put us into battle mode. I was tired, but I could do this: I sat down on the floor of her room, closed my eyes, and breathed. I focused all of my attention, as best I could, on *this* deep breath in, and *this* long slow exhale. Instead of trying to control *her*, I worked on me. To my surprise, she got curious and asked me what I was doing. I told her, "I'm breathing and calming down. My body felt too agitated inside." She grabbed her teddy and climbed into my lap.

When we find ourselves in situations with our kids that feel chaotic, our first instinct is to make *them* calm down—to change the outside circumstances, the others, rather than ourselves. But if we confront their screaming with our own agitation and frustration, we just add fuel to the fire. We want to just make it stop. What if we calm our inner experience instead? We know that this is in our locus of control and, thanks to the magic of coregulation, it helps calm our children too.

Learning this kind of calm wasn't easy for me. I was raised in a family with many generations of intense tempers. I was surprised to learn that other cultures don't have such problems with anger and yelling. For example, parental calm is highly valued by Inuit cultures near the Arctic Circle. They see losing your temper as something that only children do, and parents face all manner of immature behaviors from their children with unflappable calm. In her book, *Hunt, Gather, Parent*, Michaeleen Doucleff explains how the Inuit *show* their children how to be calm by being calm themselves:

"Whenever children are upset—crying and screaming—the parents say very few words (words are stimulating). They make very few movements (movement is stimulating). And they show very little expression on their faces (again, emotion is stimulating). Parents aren't timid or fearful. They still have a confidence about them. But they approach the child the way you might approach a butterfly on your shoulder: Gently. Slowly. Softly."

This is easier said than done if you weren't raised by Inuit parents. My autopilot reaction was always yelling, demanding, or defensiveness. Yet I wanted to make it easier for my daughters. I didn't want them to have to struggle with their reactivity the way I have. I wanted to model calm.

How do we become calm if it was never modeled for us? It takes intention, practice, and self-compassion.

What do you want to model for your kids? Do you want to model yelling, demanding, and controlling? Likely not. So get behind the intention to model calm. If you have a parenting partner, talk with them about this intention. Write it down. Remind yourself of it daily for a while.

Then practice. If you've developed a regular meditation practice, you're practicing calm (almost) every day. Good for you!

Here's another way to practice in those difficult moments:

Be a Calm Mountain

When your child is agitated and hyperactive, they may need to "borrow" your calm. They need your help to coregulate their feelings. Follow this process to become a calm mountain:

1. **Accept your child's feelings/state.** Say to yourself, *It's okay that they feel ________* [*wild, excited, upset*]; *it's okay for them to have this experience.*

2. **Sit down and breathe.** Be still. If it helps, close your eyes and touch a hand to your heart. Imagine that your body is as solid and stable as a mountain. Take deep, slow breaths in and out.

3. **Tell yourself you are a mountain.** As you breathe in, say to yourself, *Breathing in, I am like a mountain.*

As you breathe out, say to yourself, *Breathing out, I feel solid.*

4. **Repeat as needed.** Give yourself some time to sit there, letting go of expectations. Even if your child does not spontaneously calm down, your response will be more skillful for your having calmed your nervous system and engaged your whole brain.

Finally, as you practice being calm, offer yourself *compassion*. You're not going to be perfect at this! Being a normal human being (not a robot), you'll likely lose your cool and yell sometimes—even if practicing calm is your intention. That's okay. You're not alone in this. When you offer yourself compassion for those mess-ups, you'll be better able to try again.

Take action: Write "Breathing in, mountain. Breathing out, solid" on sticky notes and place them around the house strategically to remind yourself to practice in moments you want to be calm this week.

33

How Can I Handle Misbehavior?

With mindfulness, we become more attuned to our children, ourselves, and the needs of our situations. We become better able to regulate ourselves and our children simultaneously. —Shauna Spiro and Chris White

Mindful Parenting member Sonia described how her two-year-old was hitting her older brother. She was distressed because she hadn't modeled this behavior, she didn't want to "feed" the misbehavior by giving it attention, and in her mind she was spinning out a future: Would her child become a sociopath if this continued? Was her two-year-old manipulating the situation for attention? Sonia's worry was palpable.

Here in the US, we've inherited a particular cultural mindset about children—that they're always testing boundaries and even deliberately hustling us. Recently, a mom shared her memory of dropping her one-year-old off at daycare. Her daughter was crying, and another mom warned her not to pick her up or else "she will learn to manipulate you"—as a one-year-old!

We also have outrageously inappropriate expectations for kids' behavior. Even though we know that the PFC, which acts to inhibit impulses, isn't fully developed in humans until the early twenties, we expect preschoolers to fully control their behavior and feelings.

These unhelpful ideas about children have no basis in science, so they must be cultural constructions. Instead of misguided suspicions of nefarious intent or expectations of complete self-control, I invite you to try a different idea: expect misbehavior. Expect mistakes. Expect lack of self-control. When we do this, we can stop taking our kids' behavior *personally*—it's not a deliberate attack or hustle. All kids lack self-control. All kids are rude, violent, messy, and bossy. It's not personal.

Michaeleen Doucleff writes about how the Inuits' expectations for kids are very different from ours. They expect little children to be unstable, illogical beings, not yet able to listen or understand right and wrong. Children are viewed as unreasonable, aggressive, stingy, and exhibitionist. Therefore, it's fruitless to get angry and argue with them. It's our job instead to patiently teach them and model what it means to be mature.

So what can Sonia do about her two-year-old who is hitting? How do we deal with misbehavior? Consider this: Discipline does not mean "punish;" it comes from the Latin word *discipulus*, which means disciple, student, learner, pupil. To discipline means to *teach*. So Sonia needs to ask herself, *What does my child need to learn in this moment?* Her daughter needs to learn (1) that hitting hurts others, (2) that her parents won't let her hit people or pets, and (3) she needs to learn how to express her frustration in an acceptable way. Sonia can calmly hold her daughter's hands (stopping the behavior gently) and say, "Hitting hurts! You look like you're frustrated. You can hit this pillow instead, or come tell me what's happening." She gave information, calmly acknowledged her daughter's feelings, and guided her to better ways to express her feelings.

Our children's behavior is communication—even their "bad" behavior. They are communicating their feelings, impulses, and needs. You don't need to say, "Use your words," because they communicate through their behavior. We can bring our mindful awareness to a situation to get curious about what's happening under the surface. What does your child need? Kids are driven by a yearning for security, a sense of belonging, and significance. They want to be really seen and heard. Often, simply connecting and empathetically acknowledging their feelings can relieve a situation. Other situations call for more.

How to Handle Misbehavior

Try these steps to help your child learn when they misbehave:

1. **Listen mindfully.** Calmly listen with an open mind. Listen for the feelings. Reflect back your understanding of the feelings and what happened ("You were really angry!").

2. **Ask yourself:** *What does my child need to learn in this moment?*

3. **Be a mentor.** Consider yourself the patient guide and mentor. Hold boundaries with kindness ("I can't let you throw sand") and teach your child whatever they need to learn in the moment, including

appropriate ways to express and take care of their feelings. As your child learns how to be in the world, you may need to model—do it *with* your child—at first.

4. **Debrief later.** In a calm moment, close the learning loop by talking about the situation nonjudgmentally. This is an important step! Ask questions and listen. Check the impulse to lecture. Upsets are a normal part of life, and debriefing helps everyone recover and learn from the situation.

Take action: The next time you notice misbehavior, ask yourself, *What does my child need to learn?* You're guaranteed to have a more thoughtful response!

34

How to Resolve Conflicts

Conflict in a family, openly expressed and accepted as a natural phenomenon, is far healthier for children than most parents think...family conflict may actually be beneficial to the child, always provided that the conflict in the home gets resolved constructively. —Dr. Thomas Gordon

When I was little and my brother and I argued, my parents (feeling frustrated) would yell at us to "Stop fighting and go to your rooms!" We would stomp off, resenting both each other and our parents. If I had a conflict with my dad, he grounded me. I would stew in more resentment, the chasm between us steadily widening. It felt unfair. It was always a battle. The lesson I learned from this was about arming myself for battle, not how to resolve conflicts constructively.

How was conflict resolved in your family of origin? For most of us, it was like my own upbringing: *authoritarian*—the parents always won. In a few families, parents got tired of being the enforcer and swung to the opposite end of the spectrum: *permissive*—in which the kids got their way. Both are win/lose methods of resolving conflicts: one party "wins," the other party "loses." We can get locked into this approach, and our relationship with our children becomes a power struggle, a war. We parents use our power—threats, punishments, loss of privileges, even physical aggression—over our children to "win" when they are little, but we don't foresee the unhappy effects looming in the teen years.

When you imagine your younger child becoming an adolescent, what do you picture? Many of us cringe, forecasting a future of conflict, shouting, and power struggles. We assume rebellion and hostility is inevitable. My happy news for you is that this is *not true*. While adolescents do naturally become more independent, they don't have to hate you. *Teens don't rebel against parents; they rebel against the controlling, authoritarian strategies that parents use.* They've built up a lifetime of resentment against these tactics, which don't take into account their needs. This resentment erodes the relationship, and we completely lose our influence with our child at a critically important time.

Yikes. What's the good news here? You don't have to go down that path! There's a better way to resolve conflicts that won't destroy your relationship and will teach your child more skillful means to work things out with anyone moving forward: win-win.

I teach win-win regularly in Mindful Parenting and wrote about it in *Raising Good Humans*, so head there for more details, but the essence is to change your orientation from *I need to win* to *How can we* all *get our needs met?* Children's behavior is an expression of their needs, which vary according to their development. They have needs for safety, comfort, belonging, autonomy, and so much more. We also have many needs. We can understand that conflicts arise when one party's behavior impinges on the needs of another party. Your child's need to run around and yell impinges on your need to have calm and rest. Instead of resorting to yelling and punishment, ask, "How can we get everyone's needs met?" This is the essence of win-win problem solving.

Win-win problem solving includes everyone in the conflict resolution process. We hear our children's needs and concerns and acknowledge their complaints as valid. We offer them the same respect that we wish to see from them (modeling). We express our needs as well (modeling self-respect and healthy boundaries). We listen, then we share ideas on how everyone can get their needs met. Here are some guidelines:

Win-Win Problem Solving

1. **Identify the needs**. What are each party's needs? Practice mindful listening.

2. **Brainstorm solutions.** Invite your kids to go first. Write down as many solutions as you can. Write down crazy or silly solutions to lighten it up!

3. **Evaluate the solutions.** What solutions meet everyone's needs?

4. **Make decisions** as to who will do what and by when. Write it down.

5. **Check in later.** Are the solutions still meeting everyone's needs? If not, start this process again.

For more details on this process, see *Raising Good Humans.*

We can use this process when our kids are little—even preverbal—by identifying their needs out loud. As our kids become used to the process, it can be done informally, but when you want to make a bigger impact, use a big piece of paper to write things down.

Using win-win to resolve conflicts not only teaches your child healthy conflict resolution but can shift your relationship into a mutually respectful, more conscious and connected territory during the dreaded teen years. As I write this, my daughters are twelve and fifteen. Having used these methods (imperfectly!) for years, I can report that while yes, they have their teen moments, we experience little, if any, hostility and rebellion. And we're just one of many families around the world who have close relationships in their teen years. You can join us.

Take action: Try win-win problem solving with a positive problem this week, like how to spend the weekend.

35

What Can I Do When Kids Fight?

Conflict is inevitable, combat is optional. —Max Lucado

The worst for me was bedtime. The kids were arguing. The older one doesn't want her younger sibling in her room. The younger one wants to read stories in big sister's room. It's escalating, and I'm about ready to pull my hair out or cry. Why the constant bickering? Can't they just stop?

Sibling fighting is one of the hardest things we parents have to deal with. One-on-one, we may have great relationships with our kids, but get them together and we can be miserable with the teasing and warfare. We want them to be best friends, with relationships that sustain them through adulthood, yet sibling relationships can be difficult. Mistreatment by siblings can lead to issues of worthiness that affect us for the rest of our lives!

What can we parents do? First, stop worrying about their being friends, and focus on equipping them with the attitude and skills they'll need for all of their caring relationships. The skills you're learning throughout this book will help you *model* respectful communication and conflict resolution—the most powerful form of learning. If win-win problem solving is how you resolve family conflicts, that will be their go-to method. When you empathetically listen to their upset feelings (even about a sibling), rather than dismiss them, you model compassion and respect.

You can also help cultivate positive relationships between siblings by doing whatever you can to get the good feelings flowing between them. Talk about how lucky they are to have their sibling. Let your kids overhear you telling your parenting partner about the fun and nice things they did together that day. Seek out picture books that celebrate siblings. Find activities they can do together. Instead of asking them to compete ("Who can get dressed the fastest?"), invite teamwork. Say, "You two are some team. Do you think you can get your shoes on before the timer beeps?"

For positive sibling relationships, avoid comparative praise, which can generate competition, jealousy, and rivalry. Saying "Look at how quickly Téa cleaned up. Can't you clean up like that?" just stirs resentment. Instead, try to praise your child without any reference to the sibling by simply describing what you see, feel, like, or do not like.

If you have a baby, try not to blame things on the baby. If you say "I can't play with you now, I have to nurse the baby," you may inadvertently lead your older child to hate their new sibling. It can help to play up the older child's new role as Big Brother or Big Sister, but after a time, let the roles drop, so they're not forever labeled as "the baby" or "the responsible one." Instead, practice beginner's mind to see each child as an individual.

But what about the fighting? I remember epic fights with my brother. If it got bad, Mom or Dad would intervene and solve the problem, acting as judge and jury. Yet one of us left feeling resentful because the other sibling had won. Jumping in to intervene is all too common—and then the kids never have a chance to resolve their own conflicts.

We need to give them a chance to work things out, but what if it gets dangerous? Here's a quick guide to when to intervene:

Guide to Handling Kids Fighting

(Adapted from Adele Faber & Elaine Mazlish from Siblings without Rivalry.)

First Degree: Normal bickering

Ignore it. Remind yourself that your kids are having an important experience in conflict resolution. It's okay if they do it imperfectly.

Second Degree: Fight is heating up; adult intervention might help

1. Acknowledge the heated feelings. "You two sound really mad at each other!"

2. Reflectively listen without adding judgment. Respect that this is hard for them. "Sounds like you want to have Bear sit at the bottom, and you want Bear to be at the top of the tower."

3. Express your confidence in them: "I know that you two can work out a solution that feels fair to both of you."

4. Leave the room.

Third Degree: Someone's about to get hurt; adult intervention needed

1. Describe what you see. "Looks like you both are really angry and about to hurt each other."
2. Set boundaries. "No hurting is allowed in our home."
3. Separate them. "Right now we all need time to cool off before we resolve this."

Fourth Degree: Someone is hurt

In this case, give attention first to the hurt child, not the aggressor. Then proceed to the Third Degree process.

Keep in mind: You can't do this perfectly—no one can. However, we can continuously aim for the goals of peace and connection in our families.

Take action: This week, take stock of how you might be contributing to sibling resentment. Are you comparing, asking them to compete, or dismissing their feelings? Are you jumping in to solve things too often? Set an intention for one action to focus on.

36

How to Connect with My Child Again

We care for another, but we really want them to be some other way. Attachment to our hopes and desires, to our subtle expectation destroys the tender space of love. Even the most benevolent expectations can feel like pressure and judgment to another. —Jack Kornfield

On the Mindful Mama podcast, I've asked many experts about what children need most from parents, and the answer is universal: unconditional love. Yet our love for our children can cause us to fear for them, which causes us to be critical and overly controlling, which makes our love feel like it has conditions. I now know that my rigid expectations for my first daughter led to rigid defensiveness on her side. My fear—my desire to control her actions and emotions—at times eroded our strong connection, the very thing that would lead her to feel safe, soothed, and at ease.

Emotional communication starts at birth because becoming close and connected is vital for our survival. Babies are closely attuned to their caretakers' emotions and responsiveness, which we communicate nonverbally through tone of voice, facial expressions, gaze, and body posture. Ideally, we are communicating our unconditional love—*I love and accept you no matter what.*

Over time, though, as children develop their own wants and needs, as their behavior interferes with our needs, we can become critical, dismissing, angry, and harsh—because parenting is *hard*! Yet sometimes our children interpret that as *conditional* love: "I love you only if…"

Conflict is normal and inevitable. Kids' behavior can be messy, destructive, loud, selfish, and aggressive. How do we communicate unconditional love in the face of this? Their behavior can be crazy-making, yet we want them to feel safe, soothed, and loved, so they can feel secure in who they are and lead a confident, resilient life. It can seem like an impossible needle to thread.

The answer is not to avoid or suppress all conflict, but what psychologists call "rupture and repair." Stress, conflict, and frustration are moments of rupture in your relationship with your child. As the adult, it's your job to repair the relationship, bringing you both back to a place of connection and attunement. We can take responsibility for our part of the struggle and apologize. As we model this process when our kids are little, they eventually learn to initiate repair on their own.

Don't let old family patterns and habits like stonewalling (ignoring or shutting down discussion) or defensiveness stop you from initiating the repair process with your child. While you might need a cooling-off period, make sure you circle back to repair. It might not be comfortable, but it's vital that we go through this process; unresolved conflicts can be toxic. If we don't talk through our challenges, children may harshly judge themselves or you. They may misinterpret your motives in a negative and destructive way.

By going through this repair process, we tell our child: *I love you no matter what. No matter what we said or did, it will always be important to me to be close to you.* We express unconditional love and set our child up with not only essential interpersonal skills, but also a sense of security and resiliency that will serve them throughout their lives.

How to Repair

1. **Apologize.** There's nothing quite as restorative as delivering or receiving a heartfelt apology. When we model a meaningful apology, our kids learn to apologize too. Don't force an apology after poor behavior. This teaches your child to be sorry they were caught, rather than sorry for the effects their actions or words had on others. All apologies should start with "I'm sorry I..."—this shows taking responsibility, rather than "I'm sorry *you* (felt that way)...," which is not authentic or effective.

2. **Forgive and let go.** As the adult, it's on you to model forgiveness. We all make mistakes! Forgive so that you can begin anew and move on.

3. **Grow and learn.** There's something for everyone to learn from a conflict. What led to the reaction? Could

something be done differently next time? And could something be done differently in response? Maybe listening more carefully, instructing less, accepting another's point of view, not having the last word, not always having to be right? In a relationship, there's always something to be learned from a conflict that helps you to continue to grow that relationship in a positive, healthy direction. Take the time to learn and process.

Take action: It's never too late to repair a past hurt in a relationship. If you have something to repair, this week take the time to talk about it with your child.

37

Why I Want to Date My Child

There are only 940 Saturdays between a child's birth and her leaving for college. —Harley Rotbart

My twelve-year-old daughter Sora and I wandered the grounds of the plant conservatory. Her arm was hooked around my bent elbow as we strolled and chatted, remembering things that had been here in the past. We'd had a meal outside in the grounds (with chocolate, of course), and soon we would sit and listen to some music in the garden. Later, at home, she thanked me for going. I went to bed feeling full in my heart—connected, loving, and at ease.

It's an ideal picture, I know (trust me, my life is not always so idyllic). Having heard about this event, and knowing that my other daughter was working that night as a lifeguard, it seemed like the perfect moment to take my twelve-year-old out on a one-on-one date. Yep, a date—just like you might go on with your spouse.

Relationships with our children are, in some ways, just like other relationships: To be strong and connected, you need to give it time and attention. Love is not just a noun, but also a verb. It's something we *do*—a practice, an active choice that we make again and again with the people closest to us. Just as a marriage can wither and become distant when taken for granted, your relationship with your child can become less connected if you don't actively choose to nurture it. So, just as relationship experts recommend scheduling dates with your life partner, it's a good idea to schedule regular dates with each child.

It may seem silly, the idea of dating your child. After all, you spend hours and hours with them—they live with you! Right now, you might simply want a break. I get that. You should have breaks—every relationship needs breathing room, and your downtime is essential to being a present parent. But you can think of a date with your child as a kind of break, from everyday responsibilities and habits of relating, from the roles, responsibilities, and to-dos. No need to lecture or teach deep life lessons on your date. It's a break from the daily grind, for having fun and connecting.

Special one-on-one time with your child strengthens your bond of love and connection. When your connection is strong, you're more attuned, and you reinforce that sense of *caring* about the other. Then parenting becomes easier: Each of you are more likely to talk openly, listen with interest, and respect each other's needs. Going on a date with your kid opens up the lines of communication, making it smoother to talk in the challenging moments.

You have fewer than a thousand Saturdays with your child between their birth and the time they'll likely leave the nest. Time is our most precious, most valuable resource, and, just as every aged person says when you have a baby, childhood goes by *fast*. We can never get our time back, so let's spend it on what is most precious to us: our relationships with those we love.

It's a good idea to schedule your date—and an *especially* good idea if you and your kid are having a hard time right now. But we can date our kids no matter what state our interactions are in.

How often should you take your child on a date? The specific logistics of your family matter quite a bit here: You will go out less often if you have six kids than just one. Anything from once a month to several times a year works well. Here are some ideas for what to do:

Take Your Kid on a Date: Twenty Ideas

1. Go out to breakfast.
2. Go roller skating or ice skating.
3. Enjoy ice cream or milkshakes.
4. Go for a hike or camping trip.
5. Take your child to a fancy restaurant.
6. Go to the zoo or aquarium.
7. Surprise your child by picking them up from school and going to lunch.
8. Take a fitness class together.
9. Go to a museum.
10. Take a cooking class together.

11. Go for manicures or pedicures.
12. Go for a bike ride.
13. See a play at a local theater.
14. Play mini golf.
15. Get seats at your favorite spectator sport.
16. Go to a rock-climbing gym.
17. Go to a concert.
18. Go to a bookstore.
19. Go see a movie.
20. Go to an arcade or bowling.

Take action: In the next few weeks, talk with your child and put a date on the calendar. Ask what they would like to do, or suggest your own idea. Have fun!

38

My Home Undermined My Parenting

When [children] are young and growing, we adults can offer the protection of more time and ease, less speed and clutter. We can be the stewards of our child's home environment, setting limits and saying no to too many choices, too much stuff. —Kim John Payne

There were toys everywhere, again. I turned from the kitchen to find my two-year-old daughter had pulled everything out, and I mean everything: all the blocks, stuffed animals, dolls, books, and plastic toys were scattered around the living room, willy-nilly. When it was time to clean up, just like the last time, she freaked out and had a tantrum. Was every day of parenting going to be like this?

Happily, just like you, I was reading a helpful book that offered a radical suggestion: Get rid of half the toys, then get rid of half again. Okay, Simplicity Parenting: game on!

The next day I went at it in a decluttering frenzy. I donated a bunch of toys and put most of what was left in bins in a closet. I left out only a small selection: some stuffed animals, a single puzzle, a basket of blocks, and a basket of scarves. They were spaced out on the shelves, with only about six toys and puzzles out. As we walked home, I worried about her reaction. She walked in, I held my breath, and…she loved it!

She thought her space was wonderful and proceeded to play intently by herself for two hours. I was flabbergasted.

In our Western "more is better" culture, most of us have too much stuff. Advertising campaigns tell us that our child's happiness comes from having more, more, more. Our generous parental impulses to provide well for our kids' well-being are manipulated by marketing. We don't realize that all of this stuff leads to stress and a sense of overwhelm for kids. It's too much for them to easily take care of, and they don't value what they have. Think about it: If your child has a pile of toys, how much do they value that one item in the middle?

Unless you are a master organizer, a cleanup drill sergeant, or your child's full-time personal maid, the glut of toys and stuff leads to a cluttered, chaotic environment. We know from research that clutter leads to higher levels of the stress hormone cortisol in adults (Ferrari and Roster 2017). Kids, too, feel the stress. Their behavior often reflects the disorder around them. Happily, simplifying can help. In one study, 68 percent of kids diagnosed with ADD went from clinically dysfunctional to clinically functional in four months of a regime that included simplifying stuff, schedules, and media.

Fewer toys and a tidier environment give kids a sense of ease, openness, and relaxation. Less stuff promotes creativity—the scarf becomes a cape, the roof of a shelter, a sling, a bandage, and more. Less stuff is less distracting, promoting a longer attention span. With less, they learn to value what they have more, take better care of their things, and more easily learn the habit of cleaning up because it's not so overwhelming. It makes life with kids easier. Kids don't miss the clutter any more than you do.

How much should you declutter? I give guidelines about what toys to declutter in *Raising Good Humans*, and Kim John Payne goes into it in depth in *Simplicity Parenting*, so please check out those resources. However, I invite you to picture your child's spaces with a clear floor, six to ten books arrayed invitingly, four to eight toys and puzzles spaced out on the shelves, a basket with blocks covered by a scarf, a few stuffed animals and dolls, and some art supplies available. Everything is easily accessible and easy to put away because every item has its spot. There are no bins or spaces under the bed or desk bursting at the seams.

How will your child react to your having radically decluttered their toys? Chances are you will be surprised at their delight. In Mindful Parenting, hundreds of families have done this, and I've yet to hear a story of an upset child—the vast majority are truly thrilled. Of course, be careful to not get rid of any beloved, essential toys. When in doubt, keep these in a bin in the basement for a few months before donating them. Put the toys you want to keep, but don't want out all the time, away in a closet, so every other week you can rotate the toys, allowing your child to get excited about something new.

Less stuff means more ease, greater creativity, and a greater focus on relationships. It creates an environment that promotes both your and your child's mental and emotional well-being.

Take action: Declutter your child's toys so that you only have out what they can put away by themselves in five minutes.

39

Less Stress, More Ease at Home

In the day's most regular rhythms, its high notes—the meals and bathtimes, the playtimes and bedtimes—young children begin to see their place in the comings and goings, in the great song of family. —Kim John Payne

One year we packed up our tent to go to a three-day folk festival—a wonderful, family-friendly event. We did have a lot of fun, but it was hard for my youngest daughter, around two at the time, because we were way off the regular schedule and she couldn't nap. She fussed and whined, and finally at one point broke down in screams and wails for an embarrassingly long time. Eventually, she fell asleep on my husband's lap. Then his legs went to sleep too and we had to wake her up. Her big sister helped smooth things over by providing an ice cream cone just as little sister's eyes opened.

I wanted a go-with-the-flow lifestyle, taking my chillaxed (wishful thinking here) children to lots of fun events, but unfortunately my vision and reality didn't mesh. Irregular schedules and events could be fun, but they also added an element of chaos and stress to our lives, which anyone who has taken small children on "vacation" knows. My kids seemed to do better on down days at home. In fact, they thrived on *predictability*—how boring! Yet all children need it, because it supports feelings of safety and security, so let's use a better term: rhythm.

Young children have very little control over their lives. Since they don't have our big-picture adult view, they don't yet understand the schedule or the seasons of life. They look to the rhythm of their daily and weekly life to understand the world. First we wake up, then we eat breakfast, then we clean up, after lunch we rest, and so on. Children know that Mommy or Daddy will always come home before dinner or after preschool. We have pancakes every Sunday. This kind of predictable rhythm gives children a sense of safety and security, as well as warding off many kinds of behavior difficulties, because children know what to expect. We adults also benefit. A busy, fly-by-the-seat-of-your-pants life can feel like a stressful game of whack-a-mole. When we have more consistency, our own sanity and ease thrive.

Bringing a sense of regular rhythm into your life may sound like an insurmountably large ask,. Many of us work irregular hours, deal with ex-spouse childcare sharing, or may simply be way too busy. Yet those circumstances make kids' need for the stability of rhythm all the more acute.

Think of rhythm as cycles of predictability: We start to connect one habit with another until we have a regular rhythm. In our house, naptime (as they grew older, rest/quiet time) was after lunch, and that anchored our day. Because this was such a steady, expected daily cadence, it was easier. Sleep—bedtimes, waking up, and nap times—can become familiar pillars of the day when we approach it in a routine, predictable manner. Studies show that kids who follow regular bedtime routines go to sleep earlier, sleep longer, and wake up less in the night, and those benefits help children years later (Hale et al. 2011).

Family meals are a tried-and-true anchor for family life. Don't get into the habit of eating separate meals from your children! As messy and chaotic as they can be when they're little, family meals can be an important touchstone of connection as they get older. The simple ritual of coming together to eat, listen, and talk strengthens shared values and beliefs.

I learned one of my favorite ways to create predictability in our home from Kim John Payne's *Simplicity Parenting*: a weekly meal rhythm. Each night of the week we would have a different base ingredient for our meals. Monday was pizza, Tuesday was rice night, Wednesday pasta, and so on. It made life so much easier because it wasn't as intensive as full-meal planning, but I knew how I would shape the meal. The girls came to know the weekly schedule through the meal nights—if tonight was rice night, tomorrow they could expect pasta. We had fewer mealtime battles, and it added to the sense of ease and security for the kids.

The goal with rhythm is to reduce the amount of surprise in your child's life. A super-simple way to do that is by previewing the day: Each morning, talk to your child about what is going to happen in their day.

As children become familiar with the rhythm of your household, there can be fewer conflicts and less anxiety for everyone.

They will know what to do and can do it without argument, and eventually without instruction. With a basis in the security of regular rhythms, your child's ease, confidence, and cooperation will grow.

Take action: Talk to your parenting partner about implementing some rhythm in your days and weeks. Perhaps it's as simple as a weekly movie night or screen-free Sunday. Choose something and stick to it, letting time make it a habit.

40

How Not to Make Life Harder for Myself

We must, therefore, quit our roles as jailers and instead take care to prepare an environment in which we do as little as possible to exhaust the child with our surveillance and instruction. — Maria Montessori

When I enrolled my almost-two-year-old daughter in the neighborhood Montessori school, I loved the classroom: the adorable little chairs and tables, sinks so low to the ground, short cubbies and shelves—everything sized for a toddler. Soon I came to be even more impressed with the gentle buzz of quiet busyness that the twenty-five toddlers made—no screaming, crying, or yelling! How was it possible that my one daughter was louder at home than a whole classroom full of toddlers? How was this calm, productive classroom possible with so many toddlers?

At the time, I didn't realize that an "adorable" toddler-sized environment was a big factor in facilitating the ease and concentration I saw in the kids. In Montessori, they call it the "prepared environment," and it's a key feature of the method. It means that the entire space is beautifully configured for children to do things independently. Before Maria Montessori had some built, no one had thought of having child-sized tables and chairs!

At that time, I had not put much thought into making our home more accessible for my tiny child. In fact, every day our home environment made parenting more difficult. Maggie needed me to put away her jacket, get her a cup of water if she was thirsty, and do countless other things because she couldn't do them herself. I had been promoting her dependence (face-palm). But I could help her become more capable simply by changing the environment.

Full of excitement, I went to the hardware store for some hooks and installed one about three feet off the ground for her jacket. Soon I had stools at the ready in the kitchen and both bathrooms. I put a small spray bottle of vinegar and water with a rag in a basket on the floor to help with cleaning up. I put a sturdy little pitcher of water with small jam-jar glasses available for her to reach in the kitchen.

How did it work? There were some adjustments and certainly some spills (which provided opportunities to learn how to clean up), but little by little, she took care of more things by herself. Now, when she complained that she was thirsty, I reminded her that she could get herself some water. I learned that little kids can do much more than we give them credit for, if only the environment allows it, and it feeds their self-confidence.

Promote Independence at Home

In the kitchen:

- Add step stools to allow your child to help at the counter.
- Free a bottom drawer for your child-sized tools.
- When you cook, think ahead about the different activities that your child could help you with: snapping the green beans, pouring the milk into the batter, breaking an egg, cutting with a child-safe knife...
- Have a sturdy pitcher and cups at a reachable height for your child to get their own drink.

In the bedroom:

- Swap the cot for the floor bed.
- Display two or three outfits next to your child's bed for them to choose from.
- Add a second, lower bar in the closet that your child can reach to hang clothes.

In the rest of the house:

- Add a coat hook at your child's level.
- Add step stools in the bathroom.
- Put things you want your child to be able to reach in baskets on the floor.
- Have a child-sized table and chairs available.

- Consider getting child-sized real tools (not toys) like a broom, mop, snow shovel, and so on so your child can help out. The For Small Hands website is a great resource for these!

As you make your home more accessible to your child, don't make the big mistake that I did: suddenly expecting your child to do things independently *all the time*. Wait a sec, isn't that the goal? Not really. Learning is a gradual process, and children's mental and emotional capacity is not the same as their physical capacity. Children learn by first watching, then doing it *together with you*, then doing it while you watch, then finally doing it independently. There's no set timetable for this process. Expect mistakes, spills, messiness, and immaturity, but don't give up. Your sanity and your child's capability and confidence are worth it.

Take action: Consider your home from your child's perspective. Can they put away their things, pour themselves some water, and wash their own hands? If not, start to make your home accessible to promote their independence!

41

Take a Break

Almost everything will work again if you unplug it for a few minutes, including you. —Anne Lamott

I can't tell you how many times I've talked to a parent (almost always a mom) in the Mindful Parenting membership about the challenges she's having with reactivity—not responding the way she wants to, or losing it with her kids—when I hear that she hasn't had a break from her kids in two weeks, three months, even *years*. Then I know that exactly none of the advice she's asking about will stick—her challenge will keep coming up until she takes a break (or several) from her kids.

Our relationship with our kids is like all of our relationships: It needs breathing space. We are better parents when we have regular breaks from our kids. First, consider space: In all relationships, if we are with each other day in and day out (including nights!), for weeks and months on end, we will inevitably irritate, annoy, and chafe at each other's presence. We smother each other. We lose all perspective, finding it hard to see each other with fresh eyes and appreciate each other's good qualities. I recently walked with a friend who spoke with such perspective and heartfelt love about her nine-year-old…who happened to be spending a week with Grandma. She was out of the trenches and could see the big picture.

You might think, *Isn't the number one thing my child needs my presence—me, here, mind, body, and heart fully in the present moment, seeing and hearing them?* Yes, that's true. But your child doesn't need that *all* of the time. Children need practice with independence and making relationships with other loving caregivers. They also need to experience a world in which their needs aren't always met right away. That's how they learn *resilience*—that life can be challenging, and they will still be okay. They learn that it's safe to have time apart and that you always reunite.

You may ask, what about giving my child a secure attachment? It's a myth that a secure attachment requires one parent to be on call twenty-four hours a day for a child—indeed, it's harmful for that parent. It leads to burnout, resentment, and frequently losing it. If at all possible, it shouldn't be *just you*. It really does take a village to raise a child. It takes you, your parenting partner (if you have one), family members, teachers, babysitters, and the childcare community. The only way humans evolved to manage such high-needs young is by using community support.

Regular breaks from your kids and parenting make you a better parent. You know that raising children is demanding of your time, your attention, and your patience—that to do it well takes a lot of time and energy. Where does that energy come from? You are not a bottomless cup of giving, and you don't have to be. Taking regular breaks revives you so you can come back to your children with more patience, more fun, and more calm, curious attention. Neither ourselves or our children thrive when we are overstretched, exhausted, and burned out.

Not only will some space make you a better parent, but, honey, you deserve it! You deserve regular breaks to be not just the role of parent, but to be *you*. You deserve time to dedicate to your health, your fulfillment, and, dare I say, your *pleasure*. You are allowed to have fun without your children (and that will help you become a better parent)! Breaks give you the freedom and time to be yourself; then your children don't feel an unspoken pressure to be the sole source of your joy and fulfillment. It's too much pressure on them! Give yourself time to be you, to seek your own actualization outside of parenting so that when you are with your children, you can simply be with them.

What kind of breaks are right for you? If you have an infant, you can leave your child in the arms of another loving caretaker and simply take a walk by yourself, visit with a friend, or take a class. As they get older, take more time. See what feels right for you, and know that it's okay to feel a little tug at your heart as you take your leave. Regularly take time to meet your needs outside of parenting. It's safe to have your child miss you and be reunited. They will experience life relating to other loving caregivers, life independent of you. You will remember who you are outside of the role of parent and come back to your child with more energy to give.

Take action: Do you regularly take time for yourself? If not, talk with your parenting partner and/or alloparents (caregivers besides biological parents) to find ways to incorporate regular breaks away from your child.

42

Downtime for Everyone

If we do not allow for a rhythm of rest in our overly busy lives, illness becomes our Sabbath—our pneumonia, our cancer, our heart attack, our accidents create Sabbath for us. —Wayne Muller

The pressure on parents right now is immense. Not only are we supposed to provide the perfect, nurturing home, but we're also falling behind if our kids aren't immersed in language classes or violin by the time they're five. There are so many activities that are good for our kids: swimming, jiu jitsu, piano, Russian math...that we feel like we're falling behind or even negligent if our children aren't doing several different classes. The pressure starts when they're babies and just keeps going, until we find ourselves living congested lives. Parents of kids in middle and high school eat dinner on the road between gymnastics and band practice, feeling like there's never enough time.

Why are so many of us living jam-packed, stressful lives? You may be working multiple jobs to make ends meet while also caring for your child. You may be worried about missing out. Your busyness may be a product of the digital age—never being able to "turn off," or dealing with the blurred lines between work and life. With the ubiquitous smartphone, we are never disconnected, living in a state of mental arousal and distraction. But what if we put up some boundaries around this "too much" world and gave ourselves and our kids some space?

I'm not suggesting that you go live in the woods and completely disengage from life—just to restore some desperately needed balance. We all need downtime to be able to process life. If we're ever going to have a chance to see clearly, appreciate our experiences, and be present for each other, we must provide stretches of pause.

Here's a shocking little secret: You don't have to be productive all the time. You don't have to drive to every practice. You don't have to say yes to every event. You don't have to volunteer if your time is free. You don't have to sign up for the travel team. Both you and your child can and should have downtime and boundaries around what you'll say yes to. You can and should invite the feeling of rest and relaxation into your life. Ironically, when you do, you'll do better at the essential tasks! Research has shown that the busy feeling actually leads to worse performance on tasks (DeDonno and Demaree 2008). But this isn't about performance; it's about being present for the miracle that you are walking around on this planet, and witnessing your child experiencing this life too.

When we pack our lives with events and to-dos, we have no energy to be here for our lives. Overscheduled days lead to overwhelmed, stressed-out parents and kids who are prone to anxiety, snapping at each other and having meltdowns. Even if it's back-to-back fun and amusement, we can't enjoy it without breathing space to process. We need downtime. Kids need downtime, and they need *us* to protect their downtime for them. Here are some ways:

How to Be Less Busy

1. Start seeing busy as a choice. It may be a habit or social conditioning. Regardless, it's within your power to change.

2. Take a sabbath (a day of abstinence from work). This may be one full day or afternoon a week where you don't check email or social media, don't work, and don't schedule much.

3. When your kids are young, do only one activity or sport per season. When they're older, ask them to get rides to some of their activities.

4. Don't multitask. Do one thing at a time. You will feel less busy and become more productive.

5. Plan downtime into your schedule. If you have a big event coming up, block off the next few days afterward for downtime.

6. Remind yourself, *There's more than enough time for everything important.* Use this as a mantra when you find yourself rushing.

Life is precious, and kids grow quickly. If we are doing too much, we won't be fully present to experience it, and our kids will lose the space and time to be a kid.

Take action: I dare you to take one thing off of your calendar and reserve some downtime. What can you say no to?

43

Kids Need This More Than Piano, Screens, and Sports Combined

Children need the freedom and time to play. Play is not a luxury. Play is a necessity. —Kay Redfield Jamison

When Sora was three, I helped her out of the pool at the end of her swimming class. Nearby another mom was hurrying her son along at a frantic pace—his tumbling class started soon, and they had to hustle. Many of us are like this mom, filling all of our children's moments with extracurricular activities. It's not because we think our child's going to be the next Serena Williams, but because we feel pressured to give them a range of opportunities. *Everyone else's kid is in pee-wee soccer; my child will be missing out!* Unfortunately, this pressure is depriving kids of something they need much more: *free play.*

You know what free play is. Picture kids riding bikes, climbing trees, making a fort with friends, playing pretend, or acting out a play with siblings. It's kids choosing what they want to do and how they want to do it without any adults directing the activity. Free play allows children to stretch their imaginations, solve problems, and process their world. It's the essence of childhood, and it's under attack.

I met my longest lifelong friend when I was just four years old, playing by myself on my street. It's hard to imagine today! Free play time has been in decline because of (largely unfounded) fear for our kids' safety, ubiquitous screens, and a focus on academic learning. It's rare to find children rolling down hills, climbing trees, and spinning in circles just for fun. Recess times have shortened due to increasing educational demands, and children rarely play outdoors because of liability issues and our hectic schedules.

These days it's hard to find groups of kids outside at all, and if you do, they will likely be wearing team uniforms. While formal, adult-structured activities have a place (they are especially beneficial for older kids and adolescents), little kids benefit hugely from creating their own rules. Pick-up sports and made-up games teach kids vital life lessons: how to keep everyone happy to keep the game going; how to settle conflict; and that having fun really *is* more important than winning.

As free play has decreased (Entin 2011), children's mental, physical, and emotional health problems have risen—anxiety, depression, obesity, and diagnoses of ADHD in kids are on the rise (Mesure 2014). Researchers argue that the decline of free play, particularly outdoor free play involving some risk, is a major cause of the high rates of depression and anxiety in middle and high school students (Sandseter and Kennair 2011).

Through free play, children learn to resolve conflicts and self-regulate their emotions, challenge themselves physically, and gain self-confidence. Playing outside in nature and risky, adventurous play are particularly beneficial to children's mental health. In risky play, kids get a little afraid and practice keeping their heads while experiencing that fear. They learn that they can manage their fear, overcome it, and come out alive. In rough-and-tumble play they may get angry, as one player may accidentally hurt another. But to continue playing, to continue the fun, they must overcome that anger. If they lash out, the play is over. This is the *emotion regulation* theory of play (LaFreniere 2011).

Enforced stillness, by either teachers or screens, isn't healthy, natural, or beneficial for kids. They *need* free play for their personal, social, physical, mental, and emotional development. Here's how you can support it:

Support Free Play

In your family:

- Limit screen time. It's immersive and addictive—use it sparingly!
- Cut back on extracurricular activities and organized sports for little kids. Stick to one kiddie class or sport per season.
- If your child complains that they are bored, remember, it's not your job to be their entertainer. Say, on repeat, "There's something to do right around the corner," until you are so boring that they find something else to do.

- Get your child outside for three hours every day, weather and season permitting. Natural environments challenge, yet calm the senses.
- If your child's climbing high, instead of saying "Get down" ask "How does that feel to be up so high? Does that feel safe? Is there something to hold onto?" or "What's your exit strategy?" If you feel nervous, spot your child.

In the community:

- Choose and advocate for play-based kindergarten.
- Support legislation that allows kids to walk to the playground and other kid destinations on their own. Advocate for crosswalks and other pedestrian-friendly measures.
- Get involved with the Let Grow movement and encourage your school to adopt a Let Grow program (LetGrow.org)
- Get together with other families at a park, and let the kids play while you talk to the adults. Don't hover.

Take action: Pick an item from this list and practice it this week. Do you worry about safety? Visit https://LetGrow.org and learn more about the research and benefits of free play.

44

How Can I Create Helpful Kids?

When parents continue to dress their children after the age of three, they are robbing them of developing a sense of responsibility, self-sufficiency, and self-confidence. They are less likely to develop the belief that they are capable. —Jane Nelsen

Maggie is playing, so now's the time to sneak off and start making dinner. If I go quietly, she won't notice me, right? Wrong! And she wants to be with me in the kitchen. Making dinner would be a thousand times easier if she would just go play.

I repeated this scene endlessly when my daughter was little, shooing her away to be able to make dinner. Fast forward to today, and more often than not she's upstairs in her room while dinner's being made, not exactly raising her hand to help.

If I wanted my children to help around the house, I was going about it in the wrong way. When they were little, I didn't want them to get involved in tasks because their "help" created a bunch of extra work for me. Then when they were older and more capable, I forced them to help, causing them to resist and resent doing work around the house.

I did some things right: I expected them to help, I encouraged independence, and I provided stools! However, much further down the line, I learned the secrets of getting children to help from Michaeleen Doucleff, a journalist and mother of a spirited, challenging three-year-old, who happened upon some extraordinarily helpful Mayan children while researching another story. She went back to learn more and ended up writing an insightful book about various parenting practices of indigenous people: *Hunt, Gather, Parent.*

In our conversation, she pointed out that we regularly shoo small children away when there's work to be done. We may give them some screen time to keep them out of the way. This inadvertently tells them they are not supposed to help. Instead of being a contributing member, they have special, VIP status; parents do the work while they get entertained. During that critical preschool time when they really want to help and "do it myself," we not only *don't* encourage it, we actively *discourage* kids' helpfulness.

Yet it's possible to raise very helpful kids. In Mayan families, Doucleff saw a twelve-year-old daughter come downstairs and, seeing dirty dishes in the sink, go clean those dishes *without any prompting whatsoever from her parents*. If you have a tween, this may sound fantastical, but I assure you it's true. How do we get our kids to be helpful like that? It's all about encouraging, but never forcing, helpfulness from the very beginning.

Cultivate Helpfulness in Your Child

When your child's a baby:

"Wear" your child in a carrier or have them nearby while you cook and do chores. This normalizes being a part of helping.

When your child's a preschooler:

As much as you can, accept and encourage their "help" with jobs around the house. This doesn't have to be 100 percent of the time, but keep the goal that helping should be a natural part of being a member of the family.

Ask your child to watch you first, then offer them little jobs. A young child can wash a potato or hand you some pasta to put in the pot. They can help wipe up a mess.

Slow down and allow ample time to get things done with little kids.

Expect mistakes! Just gently guide your child back to being productive. This will happen multiple times. It's just part of the process.

Request help. Ask your child to hold the door while you take out the garbage, or to run and fetch something for you.

Cultivating help at all ages (including adult partners!):

> Focus on working together. Invite and initiate helping on tasks that you can do together, like preparing dinner. Ask everyone to clean up together as a family. You may also have individual chores.
>
> Keep requesting help! Continue to invite your kids to help, even if they decline at first. Think patient persistence.

If your child is already older, don't despair! You can and *should* start to cultivate helpfulness at any age. Chores are life skills that kids need to become adults. As I finish up this chapter, I'm recovering from Covid-19, which my husband and I had at the same time. We were quarantined together while my daughters, now twelve and fifteen, completely ran the house. For four days they made the meals, did the dishes, fed the cats and dog, and did all the chores it takes to run a house on their own. They had the skills they needed, and they pitched in without grumbling. Kids can be far more capable than we expect.

Take action: Invite your child to help you prepare some meals this week. Allow extra time, and practice patience!

45

Love More, Care Less

We cannot control our children. We can only create the conditions for them to rise. What this means is that we need to stop expending our energy on trying to control who they are and how they turn out in the future. The real challenge is to keep our eyes on the parameters that are truly under our control—ourselves, and the way the home functions. —Shefali Tsabary

My older daughter is highly sensitive, which meant that she was *really* fussy as a toddler. When she was cranky, I would get anxious that I wasn't "doing it right." Then I would try to control her behavior, believing that if I could produce a certain outcome, I was doing something right. She balked against my efforts to "make" her do anything, refusing to be manipulated, becoming even crankier, which deepened my anxiety. It was a vicious cycle.

We love our children so much that we care enormously about their behavior. We want the best for them, which, consciously or not, translates into wanting them to *be* the best—to be smart, adorable, physically adept, and helpful—so they will do well in this world. Our concern, our care can translate into too much control and manipulation, hovering over them, making sure that their every action and statement is approved of. Our love can cause us to care too much. And care can alchemize into parental anxiety suspended over our children's lives.

For children to grow and thrive, they need us to *love them more and care less*. Children need space to be themselves, to make mistakes, be stupid, be silly and unskillful. They need time when their actions aren't performative because they're under the worrying gaze of their parent. They need stretches of autonomy when they decide what to do and how to be, so that they can get to know themselves. When we give kids that space, they learn what interests them, what drives them, and how to walk to the beat of their own drum.

When my children went to Montessori school, I learned one of their guiding phrases: "follow the child." The idea is that children learn something the most when they are *interested*, rather than our imposing what and when they should learn. From this and my mindfulness practice I started to realize the value of stepping away from being the "controller," to instead being the curious observer of my child. When I could get into a space of curiosity rather than judgment, when I could let her be more, I thrived as a mom, and we flowed together. But when I was anxious or irritated, I tried to rigidly control her. Then I felt out of flow, out of connection.

We want this kind of rigid control because of fear. The ego—your sense of a separate self—is fighting for your survival. It wants to shore up your self-image; it seeks validation and safety in the wider world. Fear drives this desire for control. When our child makes a mistake or behaves unskillfully, we may worry that she'll never get along with others, or he'll always be dependent. These fears are largely unconscious as we hover over our children, managing every statement or action.

Loving our children more and caring less means letting them *own* their life. It means asking questions and becoming more support staff than director. Yes, as the parents, we are the captains of the family ship, but we don't have to *micromanage* our kids' lives. What does caring less look like? Just closing the door when their room is messy rather than picking a fight. Creating a supportive environment for them to do homework, but letting the responsibility for homework be theirs. Giving kids some time to get chores done rather than yelling for it to happen right now. Drawing the line at just one organized activity for our twelve-year old, but letting her choose it.

As Shefali Tsabary says in the chapter epigraph, we *can't* control our children—it's a fruitless, anxiety-inducing endeavor. What can we control? In parenting it boils down to ourselves and our environment. When we relinquish the idea of control, we can focus our attention on things that have far more lasting impact: creating a close, connected relationship, and *modeling* the kind of behavior we'd like to see.

Take action: Are you attempting to control most of your child's actions? If so, take this week to step back, practice some restraint, and instead observe with curiosity.

46

I'm Not Passing Those Thoughts On to My Kids!

Anytime you're feeling stressed, anxious, or depressed, ask yourself, "What story is my mind telling me now?" Then once you've identified it, defuse it. —Russ Harris

I remember as a kid watching my mom look at herself in the mirror. She must have been feeling pretty bad, because she had a disgusted expression and said to herself, "I'm so ugly." It was heartbreaking to witness. Later on, in my late teens and early twenties, I, too, looked at myself in the mirror and told myself I was ugly. Her inner voice became my own, and I repeated that pattern. It took many years to heal.

I'm not throwing my mother under the bus here—we all have an inner critic, and she happens to be a wonderful, loving, and self-aware person—but for everyone, that voice in your head can be intensely critical and downright nasty. I tell this story to let you know that at some point or other—whether you want it to or not—*your inner voice comes out.* Your kids will eventually hear your inner voice. If you don't want your kids to absorb the hostility of the inner critic, it's imperative to interrupt this habit.

You may expect me to suggest telling yourself the *opposite* of that critical thought, but that can backfire. Research on positive affirmations has shown that they can boost you *if* you're already in a good mood, but if you're feeling low (when you might actually need a boost), they can actually make things worse (Wood, Perunovic, and Lee 2009). Turns out that if you tell yourself that you're wonderful when you think that you're terrible, you'll argue that positive thought away. However, there are powerful tools to shift that inner voice. You can first *interrupt* those thoughts, then offer yourself some *compassion*. These tools, practiced consistently, will rewire your neural pathways and change the voice you pass on to your child.

According to Russ Harris, physician, therapist, and author of *The Happiness Trap*, the problem is not with our negative thoughts, but that we *believe* these thoughts are true. We have become "fused" with negative, critical thoughts that leave us feeling helpless. Therefore, we have to *defuse* them—or get a bit of distance from those thoughts.

Defuse Negative Thoughts

1. **Notice the toxic thoughts.** Mindfulness will help with this. We can't change what we're not aware of, and simply noticing interrupts the habit.

2. **Preface the thought with the phrase, *I'm having the thought that…*** This interrupts the normal pattern. Let's say you think to yourself, *I'm a terrible mother.* If you add *I'm having the thought that,* it loses its power. Now it's just a thought. When you interrupt a thought like this, that little bit of space allows you to consider whether this thought is helpful or not.

The more often you interrupt that neural pattern, the less likely it is to repeat in the future. This is the brain's natural plasticity at work. Brain researchers like to say "Neurons that fire together, wire together," meaning that as you practice defusing thoughts you are creating a new, healthy pattern.

Once you've interrupted the thought, you can see how unkind this voice inside your head has been to you—you have been talking to yourself as if you were your own worst enemy! These thoughts have led to your own suffering. It's time to practice self-compassion, which includes mindfulness (awareness of the unkind thought), self-kindness, and recognizing that you're not alone—we *all* experience this. Head back to chapter 4 for a self-compassion break practice, taking a moment to consciously offer yourself kindness when you become aware of that harsh critical voice. You're starting a new habit.

As you practice defusing and offering yourself compassion, also practice some more helpful, positive thoughts. When I journal, I end each entry with two affirmations: "I am enough" and "I love and accept myself exactly as I am." Rather than taking me down, these thoughts help me stay grounded and confident—better able to be present for children's chaos.

These practices aren't just nice to do. We are changing harmful generational patterns for ourselves and for our children. They are picking up on not only your behavior and your actions, but your *mindset*. Do you want your child to see the world through a dark, cynical lens? Negative self-talk is toxic; it can leave you unable to show up for your family, adding stress to your life and everyone you touch. Don't pass that on to your children. Instead, cultivate an inner voice that helps you show up positively for your life.

Take action: What's your inner voice like? This week, practice defusing negative thoughts.

47

Childhood Is Slow

Kids don't remember what you try to teach them.
They remember what you are. —Jim Henson

When my older daughter was a toddler, I would sometimes get waves of anxiety, thinking about how to fill the long hours ahead. Caring for her by myself could leave me with an unsettling emotional combination of boredom and fear of messing up. Sometimes my answer would be to fill our day with activities, which reliably backfired as stress and chaos when both of us became overwhelmed with the schedule. I circled back again and again to this lesson: Slow down.

Slowing down is necessary—and for many of us, incredibly hard. We've been taught by our culture to get stuff done, be efficient, and achieve! By the time I became a mom I'd been practicing being fast-paced and achievement-oriented for three decades. Suddenly parenthood pitched me into a different gear. Yet I learned that slowing down was exactly what my child needed from me. It wasn't her job to speed up to the pace of adult life. It was my job to decelerate—to meet her in the naturally slower pace of childhood.

That pace is measured and gradual. Children are learning and developing in every moment, absorbing the world around them. Their brain, motor skills, and so much more are expanding, and we don't need to hurry that along. Childhood is more than just preparing for adulthood. Childhood is its own magical time, when watching an insect, pretend-playing a doctor's office, or helping Mom or Dad can utterly consume kids' attention, so they enter a state of mental flow.

We parents are the most important factors in either defending the measured pace of childhood or accelerating it. Supporting and protecting this slower pace allows children the time to learn who they are, to wonder, and to *learn to learn*. Spontaneous play—the heartbeat of a healthy child's life—can happen only if we protect children's time by slowing ourselves down. We are in the prime position to protect the magic of childhood.

Many of us miss the call to slow down. Commercial culture and inner anxiety push us to fill every moment, rushing our child from activities to lessons to theme parks. All well-intentioned, yet added up it becomes a life of *too much*. When we do too much, we inject childhood with stress and pressure to get from place to place. Children absorb our anxiety, learning the unintended lesson that the goal of life is to do as much as possible. We want to give our children great experiences, but we don't realize that children need space and (screen-free) time to *just be themselves*.

Do you get anxious with your child being bored? Don't be. Boredom is actually a safe and desirable state for your kid. Instead of dreading it, think of the "I'm bored" whine as the precursor to creativity. Don't immediately jump to solve their boredom (because it's not a problem). Instead, become so boring that your child takes off to find something better to do. My favorite way to respond to a bored kid comes from Kim John Payne in *Simplicity Parenting*: say "Something to do is right around the corner," on repeat. When you do this instead of giving your child a device, you give the gift of lifelong creativity, self-knowledge, self-confidence, and more.

For most of us, the biggest barrier to slowing down is ourselves. How can we decelerate?

Three Ideas for Slowing Down

1. **Regular mindfulness meditation practices** (see chapters 9 and 10) will settle some of your restless energy.

2. **Work out your faster energy.** Get some vigorous exercise every day—pull out the jogging stroller or the carrier for hiking, or get yourself to the gym. Burn off some of your anxious energy so that you can have more rest and ease with your child.

3. **Create a ritual to transition from efficient work mode**. If you're working full time, be deliberate about switching gears. This could include a walk up and down the street, just focusing on your breath before you enter the house. You could take three deep breaths in the car. When you enter your home, invite your child into some rough-and-tumble play for a few minutes, instead of jumping to your to-dos.

Laughter, love, connection with our children—these are available only when we are in the present moment. If we are constantly checking boxes for some future moment, when that moment gets here we won't be able to rest. Instead, *slow down*. Practice being present now, joining your child in seeing the magic all around you.

Take action: Are you rushing your child through their days? How can you practice slowing down this week?

48

Take in the Good

Optimism is the most important human trait because it allows us to evolve our ideas, to improve our situation, and to hope for a better tomorrow. —Seth Godin

A few years ago, everything happening in the world had me overwhelmed, weighed down by tragedies. So I did an experiment: I took a complete break from the news for a week. It felt strange at first, but soon I found myself refocusing on my family and my community—relocalizing. I realized that the news media is generally all of the bad news—they never focus on the less urgent, positive news. My experiment left me feeling more focused on solving problems that were within my sphere of influence. I not only felt more peaceful, I was more effective.

Our constantly connected society can leave us walking around with the weight of the world on our shoulders, with innumerable things to worry about and an endless amount of bad news to consume. We want to be informed, but it can be harmful to continually take in all that suffering and strife. It can leave you debilitated and unable to proactively solve problems that actually are within your capacity.

The images and stories we take in become part of our experience, which shapes our brain and in turn shifts the way we think. Because of our brain's negativity bias (see chapter 8), the pile of negative experiences the brain draws from can quickly outnumber the positive, which can tilt us toward cynicism, depression, or anxiety. The remedy isn't to suppress difficult experiences, but rather to foster and lean into *positive experiences* so they become a permanent part of you.

Happily, the neuroplasticity of the brain allows us to grow and change in response to new information and experiences. This is incredibly hopeful, because that means that we can choose to promote our own well-being and happiness. We can actively take in wholesome, positive experiences that can soothe us and counteract the negative. Leaning into positive experiences isn't just to feel good; it actually has far-reaching benefits, including a stronger immune system (Fredrickson 2000), lifting mood, increasing optimism, resilience, and counteracting the effects of painful experiences, including trauma (Fredrickson 2001).

Leaning into positive experiences will help you become a more present, in-tune parent to your child in three clear ways. First, when you're no longer being swept away with worry about far-off tragedies, your attention returns to your home and loved ones, where you have a substantial impact on others. Secondly, your feelings are communicable: Your child can sense when your disquiet is replaced with calm and optimism. Finally, when you stop constantly taking in negativity, you retrain your brain to look out for possibilities, opportunities, and things going *right*.

How can we take in the positive? Here are three steps adapted from Rick Hanson's *Buddha's Brain: The Practice Neuroscience of Happiness, Love, and Wisdom*.

Take In the Positive

1. **Actively look for good news.** Good things happen all around us that we don't notice or hardly register. So look for positive things, like the faces of your children and loved ones, a tree providing shade, the smell of an orange. Bring your mindful awareness to all of the positive little things!

2. **Savor the experience.** Keep your attention on the good news for five, ten, even twenty seconds. The longer you keep your awareness on it and allow it to stimulate your emotions, the more neurons fire and wire together, making it a stronger memory. Focus on how good it feels!

3. **Imagine the experience is entering deeply into your mind and body.** Like water into a sponge, visualize yourself absorbing the positive emotions, thoughts, and sensations.

I want my daughters to be resilient in the face of a difficult world. To do that, they need hope, to be able to see what's working and build on that. When we practice leaning into what's good, we role model that for our kids.

Take action: This week, notice how much you take in or focus on the negative. Are you out of balance? If so, practice intentionally taking in the positive.

49

Permission to Get Help

Mothers really were not built to raise babies not only by themselves, but with only a partner. For millions of years, a woman had much more than just her husband to help rear her young...This whole idea of "it takes a village to raise a child" is exactly how we're supposed to live. —Helen Fisher

Human babies are unusually dependent. A baby giraffe falls six feet from its mother at birth, yet is standing and walking within thirty minutes, and that *same day* it can run. Human babies require *years and years* of care before they reach maturity—far more than other mammals. How is this pattern of development possible? The answer is clear: *community*. *Homo sapiens* would not have survived and flourished with just one or two parents around. It was the support of the community and other caretakers that allowed for our extended development. So if you feel like you could use some help, that need isn't unique to our time and place in history—it's wired into our human biology.

In fact, the idea that we should be parenting by ourselves in the nuclear family is new to human history—only about the last 150 years in Western societies. Other parts of the world still wisely consider widely distributed support essential for raising children. In Mayan areas of Mexico, other moms, aunts, uncles, older kids, grandparents, and neighbors will flow in and out of the home to give new parents breaks, recognizing how much work it takes to raise a human (Doucleff 2018).

The "it takes a village idea" is encapsulated by the term *alloparenting*. According to David Lancy, anthropologist and author of *The Anthropology of Childhood*, this term conveys "the notion that all sorts of folks can step up and play what we think of as the normal parenting role—holding and comforting a child, feeding the child, cleaning the child, making sure the child is safe, protecting the child. All the various parenting roles can be distributed, and collectively those folks are called alloparents."

Unfortunately, most reading this will *not* have many alloparents. We don't have a village of relations and friends nearby to help. You may even want to skip over reading this, because it seems like an impossible dream, but don't! There are ways to bring some of this proverbial village into your life to save your sanity.

The first step to getting more support is to check your mindset: Do you believe that you *should* be able to do it all on your own? Do you think the self-sacrificing parent is noble? Examine these ideas, because they are often the basis of parents' not getting help. When we try to parent without support, not only do we suffer, but our children suffer. We are not at our best and are not offering our best. Accepting and needing the help of alloparents is natural—biologically and evolutionarily driven, in fact—so there's no need for guilt.

Instead, can you give yourself *permission* to get help? Knowing that a more balanced, grounded parent is a better parent, can you give yourself permission for the long-term health of your family? Giving ourselves permission to get support benefits everyone. Not only do parents need breaks and balance, but children thrive with multiple attachment figures in their lives.

It may not include a Mayan grandmother, but we can and should build a support network. Share the load with your parenting partner, family, and community—let them lift your burden. Once you've shifted your mindset, it's a matter of creative problem solving and persistence. You can recruit support from your extended family. You can pay for caring support. Bring in older children to take your child for walks. Ask your neighbors for help. It's not noble or helpful to go it alone. Keep the ideal in mind of having a network of caring people in your child's life, and cultivate that as you go along.

Take action: Write down a list of ten (yes, ten!) ways that you can solicit more help in caring for your child.

50

Don't Go to Bed Without This

Life is 10 percent what happens to you and 90 percent how you respond to it. —Unknown

Harvard University has been running the longest study ever on health and well-being (Curtin 2017). For seventy-five years, they've tracked a group of 456 poor men from the Boston area and a group of 268 male Harvard grads, compiling surveys, blood samples, brain scans, and more. What did they find? According to the director of the study, one factor is more important for well-being than *anything* else: "The clearest message that we get from this 75-year study is this: Good relationships keep us happier and healthier. Period."

Quality relationships are not only the most important thing for your happiness and fulfillment, but they keep you healthier as you age. In the end, you could have all the money in the world and an amazing career, but if you don't nurture those relationships, you won't be happy. Of course this includes our children, so I commend you for reading this book and prioritizing happy, healthy relationships with your kids. The most important shift of all may be to preserve the perspective that we are in a lifelong relationship with these little beings. There's more at stake than short-term control.

Perspective is essential on this journey of parenting. We won't get everything right. We *will* make mistakes. So we must give ourselves the space to see the big picture, to feel into what's working and what's not, and to course-correct if needed. We need to remember that our own peace and happiness is *the* essential foundation for this healthy relationship. The example of how we live teaches much more than our words.

I want you to remember this: You have permission to be human. You have permission to get support. And you have permission to be happy. Give *yourself* permission to be happy, because your own happiness will become your child's happiness. Your peace, your joy is palpable, transmissible to everyone in your orbit, but especially to your child, for whom you are a model for how to live. Parenting is *hard*, challenging us in the deepest ways, yet we don't always have to suffer. We don't always have to strive and work hard. Paradoxically, as we strive less, soften our laser focus on perfection, and give ourselves permission to relax, to lean into the things that bring us joy, to *play*, parenting becomes less a taxing job and more *a relationship* that supports each party.

Dear reader, give yourself permission to inject happiness into the most difficult times. Make it a priority to let yourself smile, make your child giggle, dance, and sing no matter what challenges life throws at you. I'm not asking you to cover over your difficult feelings. Feel them. And continue to turn your face toward the light. Turn your attention to your wins, to the good news, to the helpers, the healers, and the laughter. Where attention goes, energy flows: Give yourself permission to be happy, and let that energy flow to your children and beyond.

One of the best ways to water your seeds of happiness is to practice gratitude—to really make it part of your everyday life. Research shows that practicing gratitude has measurable benefits in just about every area of our lives, from physical health to mental and emotional well-being (Allen 2018). When things are looking bleak, it helps to remember what we can appreciate. I'm so grateful for my eyes to see this beautiful world and all the many colors. I have two arms with which I can hug my children. I appreciate my lack of earache or my nonbroken toe. This kind of perspective helps.

Practice Gratitude

- Each night before you go to bed, write five things you're grateful for—even just one word for each.
- Send a quick text or email expressing your gratitude to someone.
- At the dinner table, ask your family what they're grateful for.
- At bedtime, ask your child to share three things they're grateful for.
- Thank people in the community—in the checkout line, at the farmers' market.
- Silently express your gratitude for the challenges in your life that have helped you grow.

You have permission to be human. You have permission to get support. You have permission to be happy. As you use the practices in this book to build your steadiness and awareness, you'll see more clearly and freak out less—it just takes a little practice. And remember, you can always, *always* begin anew. I will be beginning anew with you.

Take action: Incorporate one of these gratitude practices into your life this week!

Recommended Resources

Books

The Awakened Family, Shefali Tsabary

Body-Brain Parenting, Mona Delahooke

How to Talk So Little Kids Will Listen, Joanna Faber and Julie King

Hunt, Gather, Parent, Michaeleen Doucleff

The Illustrated Happiness Trap, Russ Harris and Bev Aisbett

Meditation for Fidgety Skeptics, Dan Harris

Parent Effectiveness Training, Thomas Gordon

Parenting from the Inside Out, Daniel Siegel and Mary Hartzell

Peace of Mind, Thích Nhất Hạnh

Playful Parenting, Lawrence J. Cohen

Raising Good Humans, Hunter Clarke-Fields

Real Happiness, Sharon Salzberg

ScreamFree Parenting, Hal Runkel

Simplicity Parenting, Kim John Payne with Lisa M. Ross

Strange Situation, Bethany Saltman

Yardsticks, Chip Wood

*You Are Not a Sh*tty Parent*, Carla Naumburg

Websites

Mindful Parenting Membership, mindfulmamamentor.com

Mindful Parenting Teachers & Teacher Training, mindfulmamamentor.com

For Small Hands, forsmallhands.com

Insight Timer, insighttimer.com

Acknowledgments

To write a book, I need to be driven by a larger purpose. I get that through the open, honest, passionate parents I work with in Mindful Parenting and the Mindful Parenting Teacher Training. I want to acknowledge those parents, because you remind me every day of the larger purpose of this work: to transform generational patterns so that we and our children may live with greater peace, ease, and connection—so that we may think and love more clearly, bringing more understanding and compassion into the world.

I also want to acknowledge the incredible Mindful Mama Mentor team. Chelsea Gildea, Emma Greening, Lynn Weller, Yvonne Tolentino, Sam Hayden, and Alex Retsis—thank you for keeping me going with not only your help, intelligence, and organization, but especially your conviction and your humor. You've kept me writing, and I appreciate it.

Finally, I want to acknowledge the support of my family and friends. To my daughters: Your stories, your hugs, and your loving support truly buoy me. Bill, thank you for always believing in me. My friends, I appreciate your love and support more than you know.

References

Allen, Summer. 2018. "The Science of Gratitude." *Greater Good Science Center.* https://ggsc.berkeley.edu/images/uploads/GGSC-JTF_White_Paper-Gratitude-FINAL.pdf.

Arnsten, Amy F. T. 2009. "Stress Signaling Pathways That Impair Prefrontal Cortex Structure and Function." *Nature Reviews Neuroscience* 10: 410–422.

Aron, Adam R., Trevor W. Robbins, and Russell A. Poldrack. 2004. "Inhibition and the Right Inferior Frontal Cortex." *Trends in Cognitive Sciences* 8: 170–177.

Bodhi, Bhikkhu. 2013. "I Teach Only Suffering and the End of Suffering." *Tricycle: The Buddhist Review,* Winter.

Brown, Brené. 2010. "The Power of Vulnerability." *TEDxHouston.* https://www.ted.com/talks/brene_brown_the_power_of_vulnerability.

Clarke-Fields, Hunter. 2018. "The Science of Wellbeing—Dr. Dan Siegel." *Mindful Mama Podcast* 139. https://www.mindfulmamamentor.com/blog/the-science-of-presence-dr-dan-siegel-139.

Clarke-Fields, Hunter. 2019. "How to Talk to Kids—Oren Jay Sofer." *Mindful Mama Podcast* 152. https://www.mindfulmamamentor.com/blog/how-to-talk-to-kids-oren-jay-sofer-152.

Clarke-Fields, Hunter. 2021. "Are You a WEIRD Parent?—David F. Lancy." *Mindful Mama Podcast* 262. https://www.mindfulmamamentor.com/blog/are-you-a-weird-parent-david-f-lancy-262.

Curtin, Melanie. 2017. "This 75-Year Harvard Study Found the 1 Secret to Leading a Fulfilling Life." *Inc.,* February. https://www.inc.com/melanie-curtin/want-a-life-of-fulfillment-a-75-year-harvard-study-says-to-prioritize-this-one-t.html.

Davidson, Richard J., Jon Kabat-Zinn, Jessica Schumacher, Melissa Rosenkranz, Daniel Muller, Saki F Santorelli, et al. 2003. "Alterations in Brain and Immune Function Produced by Mindfulness Meditation." *Psychosomatic Medicine* 65: 564–570.

DeDonno, Michael A., and Heath A. Demaree. 2008. "Perceived Time Pressure and the Iowa Gambling Task." *Judgment and Decision Making* 3: 636–640.

Doucleff, Michaeleen. 2018. "Secrets of a Maya Supermom: What Parenting Books Don't Tell You." *National Public Radio.* https://www.npr.org/sections/goatsandsoda/2018/05/11/603315432/the-best-mothers-day-gift-get-mom-out-of-the-box.

Entin, Esther. 2011. "All Work and No Play: Why Your Kids Are More Anxious, Depressed." *The Atlantic*, October. https://www.theatlantic.com/health/archive/2011/10/all-work-and-no-play-why-your-kids-are-more-anxious-depressed/246422.

Feldman Barrett, Lisa. 2017. *How Emotions Are Made: The Secret Life of the Brain.* New York: Houghton Mifflin Harcourt.

Ferrari, Joseph R., and Catherine A. Roster. 2017. "Delaying Disposing: Examining the Relationship Between Procrastination and Clutter Across Generations." *Current Psychology* 37: 426–431.

Fredrickson, Barbara L. 2000. "Cultivating Positive Emotions to Optimize Health and Well-Being." *Prevention and Treatment* 3: 1–25.

Fredrickson, Barbara L. 2001. "The Role of Positive Emotions in Positive Psychology." *American Psychologist* 56: 218–226.

Fredrickson, Barbara L., Michael A. Cohn, Kimberly A. Coffey, Jolynn Pek, and Sandra M. Finkel. 2008. "Open Hearts Build Lives: Positive Emotions, Induced Through Loving-Kindness Meditation, Build Consequential Personal Resources." *Journal of Personality and Social Psychology* 95: 1045–1062.

Gershoff, Elizabeth T. 2013. "Spanking and Child Development: We Know Enough Now to Stop Hitting Our Children." *Child Development Perspectives* 7: 133–137.

Goldman-Rakic, Patricia S. 1987. "Circuitry of Primate Prefrontal Cortex and Regulation of Behavior by Representational Memory." In *Handbook of Physiology, Section 1: The Nervous System, Volume 5: Higher Functions of the Brain*, edited by Fred Plum. Bethesda, MD: American Physiological Society.

Goyal, Madhav, Sonal Singh, Erica M. S. Sibinga, Neda F. Gould, Anastasia Rowland-Seymour, Ritu Sharma, et al. 2014. "Meditation Programs for Psychological Stress and Well-Being: A Systematic Review and Meta-Analysis." JAMA *Internal Medicine* 174: 357–368.

Hale, Lauren, Lawrence M. Burger, Monique K. LeBourgeois, and Jeanne Brooks-Gunn. 2011. "A Longitudinal Study of Preschoolers' Language-Based Bedtime Routines, Sleep Duration, and Well-Being." *Journal of Family Psychology* 25: 423–433.

Hanson, Rick. 2009. *Buddha's Brain: The Practical Neuroscience of Happiness, Love, and Wisdom*. Oakland: New Harbinger Publications.

Kashdan, Todd B., Lisa Feldman Barrett, and Patrick E. McKnight. 2015. "Unpacking Emotion Differentiation: Transforming Unpleasant Experience by Perceiving Distinctions in Negativity." *Current Directions in Psychological Science* 24: 10–16.

LaFreniere, Peter. 2011. "Evolutionary Functions of Social Play: Life Histories, Sex Differences, and Emotion Regulation." *American Journal of Play* 3: 464–488.

Mesure, Susie. 2014. "When We Stop Children Taking Risks, Do We Stunt Their Emotional Growth?" *The Independent*, May. https://www.independent.co.uk/life-style/health-and-families/features/when-we-stop-children-taking-risks-do-we-stunt-their-emotional-growth-9422057.html.

National Research Council (US) and Institute of Medicine (US) Committee on the Prevention of Mental Disorders and Substance Abuse Among Children, Youth, and Young Adults: Research Advances and Promising Interventions. 2009. *Preventing Mental, Emotional, and Behavioral Disorders Among Young People: Progress and Possibilities*. Edited by Mary Ellen O'Connell, Thomas Boat, and Kenneth E. Warner. Washington, DC: National Academies Press.

Rusch, Heather L., Michael Rosario, Lisa M. Levison, Anlys Olivera, Whitney S. Livingston, Tianxia Wu, et al. 2018. "The Effect of Mindfulness Meditation on Sleep Quality: A Systematic Review and Meta-Analysis of Randomized Controlled Trials." *Annals of the New York Academy of Sciences* 1445: 5–16.

Saltman, Bethany. 2020. *Strange Situation: A Mother's Journey into the Science of Attachment*. New York: Ballantine.

Sandseter, Ellen B. H., and Leif E. O. Kennair. 2011. "Children's Risky Play from an Evolutionary Perspective: The Anti-Phobic Effects of Thrilling Experiences." *Evolutionary Psychology* 9: 257–284.

Shapiro, Shauna, and Chris White. 2014. *Mindful Discipline: A Loving Approach to Setting Limits and Raising an Emotionally Intelligent Child*. Oakland: New Harbinger Publications.

Straus, Murray A., and Carolyn J. Field. 2003. "Psychological Aggression by American Parents: National Data on Prevalence, Chronicity, and Severity." *Journal of Marriage and Family* 65: 795–808.

Sturge-Apple, Melissa L., Patrick T. Davies, Meredith J. Martin, Dante Cicchetti, and Rochelle F. Hentges. 2012. "An Examination of the Impact of Harsh Parenting Contexts on Children's Adaptation Within an Evolutionary Framework." *Developmental Psychology* 48: 791–805.

Swartz, Karen. 2014. "The Healing Power of Forgiveness." Interview by Lauren Sandler. *Johns Hopkins Health*, July, 6–9.

Taylor, Jill Bolte. 2006. *My Stroke of Insight: A Brain Scientist's Personal Journey*. New York: Penguin Books.

US Department of Health and Human Services, Substance Abuse and Mental Health Services Administration. 2009. "Risk and Protective Factors for Mental, Emotional, and Behavioral Disorders Across the Life Cycle." https://www.csifdl.org/wp-content/uploads/2018/07/Risk-and-Protective-Factors-Study.pdf.

Wang, Ming-Te, and Sarah Kenny. 2013. "Longitudinal Links Between Fathers' and Mothers' Harsh Verbal Discipline and Adolescents' Conduct Problems and Depressive Symptoms." *Child Development* 85: 908–923.

Whitebread, David. 2017. "Free Play and Children's Mental Health." *Lancet* 1: 167–169.

Wood, Joanne V., W. Q. Elaine Perunovic, and John W. Lee. 2009. "Positive Self-Statements: Power for Some, Peril for Others." *Psychological Science* 20: 860–866.

Yehuda, Rachel, Nikolaos P. Daskalakis, Linda M. Bierer, Heather N. Bader, Torsten Klengel, Florian Holsboer, et al. 2015. "Holocaust Exposure Induced Intergenerational Effects on *FKBP5* Methylation." *Biological Psychiatry* 80: 372–380.

Hunter Clarke-Fields, MSAE, is creator of Mindful Parenting, host of the *Mindful Mama* podcast, and author of *Raising Good Humans*. She coaches parents on how to cultivate mindfulness in their daily lives and cooperation in their families. Hunter has more thantwenty years of experience in meditation practices, and has taught thousands worldwide.

Foreword writer **Shefali Tsabary, PhD**, specializes in the integration of Western psychology and Eastern philosophy. She is an expert in family dynamics and personal development, and is author of the *New York Times* bestsellers, *The Conscious Parent* and *The Awakened Family*.

Also by Hunter Clarke-Fields

With this essential guide, you'll see how changing your own "autopilot reactions" can create a lasting positive impact—not just for your kids, but for generations to come.

ISBN 978-1684033881 / US $16.95